ROCK SPOTTER

SPOTTER

DAN GREEN

Quarto is the authority on a wide range of topics.

Quarto educates, entertains and enriches the lives of our readers—enthusiasts and lovers of hands-on living.

www.quartoknows.com

Designer: Nick Leggett
Editor: Harriet Stone

© 2019 Quarto Publishing plc

First published in 2019
by QED Publishing,
The Old Brewery,
6 Blundell Street,
London N7 9BH,
United Kingdom.
T (0)20 7700 6700
F (0)20 7700 8066
www.QuartoKnows.com

A catalogue record for this book is available from the British Library.

ISBN 978 0 7112 4121 3

Manufactured in Dongguan, China TL112018

9 8 7 6 5 4 3 2 1

Picture credits
t = top, b = bottom, r = right, l = left, m= middle, fc = front cover

ALAMY: 1 Cultura FM, 3 Greg C.Grace, 4tm Greg C.Grace, 4tm Cultura RM, 5tm Corbin17,12t Henri Koskinen, 13t Universal Images Group North America LLC/DeAgostini, 13m ASK Images, 17b The Picture Art Collection, 24t geoz, 25t Slim Sepp, 27t Valery Voennyy, 27m geoz, 29t michal812, 34t geoz, 35b Slim Sepp, 36t Alan Curtis, 36b RF Company, 37t www.sandatlas.org; 37tm Slim Sepp; 37m S.E.A. Photo; 37b BIOSPHOTO, 38b Gianni Furlan, 44t Corbin17, 45b Jeff J Daly, 51t Susan E.Degginger, 51b Universal Images Group North America LLC/De Agostini, 52t Mike Greenslade, 53m Granger Historical Picture Archive, 56t Susan E.Degginger, 60tr imageBROKER, 60l James Hughes, 60t Julie Thompson Photography, 61br PjrStudio, 65b PjrStudio, 66t PjrStudio, 69b Phil Degginger, 70t Sabena Jane Blackbird, 71br Siim Sepp, 71bl Siim Sepp, 72r Greg C Grace, 73tm Greg C Grace, 73bl Slim Sepp, 75t Björn Wylezich, 77m Mikreates, 80t Cultura RM, 84m Sabena Jane Blackbird, 84b Dorling Kindersley ltd, 85b imageBROKER, 86m The Natural History Musuem, 87m Sabena Jane Blackbird, 88t Frans Lanting Studio, 88b Dorling Kindersley ltd/, 89t ALAMY d7dnen, 92m Science History Images, 94t geoz, 96tl PjrStudio

GETTY: 5bm John Cancalosi, 7b eclipse_images, 12b DEA/ A.RIZZI/De Agostini, 17t Mark Schneider, 19b Corbis Historical, 20t DEA/C.BEVILACQUA, 21t DEA/C. BEVILACQUA, 43tr Dimitri Vervitsiotis, 48 John Cancalosi, 49m Scientifica, 62b De Agostini Picture Library, 66b DEA / G.CIGOLINI, 38t DEA/ARCHIVIO J.LANGE, 87b Wolfgang Kaehler/Lightrocket, 90t Universal History Archive/UIG, fc HIROSHI YAGI

SCIENCE PHOTO LIBRARY: 13tm Dorling Kindersley/UIG/SCIENCE PHOTO LIBRARY, 22-23m SCIENCE PHOTO LIBRARY, 35t Dorling Kindersley/UIG/SCIENCE PHOTO LIBRARY, 45tl MARK WILLIAMSON/SCIENCE PHOTO LIBRARY, 96tr SCIENCE STOCK PHOTOGRAPHY/ SCIENCE PHOTO LIBRARY, 50b Millard H. Sharp/ SCIENCE PHOTO LIBRARY, p70b SCIENCE PHOTO LIBRARY

SHUTTERSTOCK: 3l Dafinchi;RomanVX, 3m Albert Russ, 3r Breck P.Kent, 3b Alessandro Colle, 4bl Pusaltronik, 4bt Aldona Griskeviciene, 4bm arka38, 4tl Albert Russ, 4tr MarcelClemens, 5tm Bjoern Wylezich, 5bm stihii, 5b Arka38, 6t Pung, 6m canadastock, 6b vvoe, 7t Sebastian Janicki, 7m Mark Brandon, 8-9 Aldona Griskeviciene, 9t Tutpong, 9m Aldona Griskeviciene, 9b EniaB, 10t michal812, 10b www.sandatlas.org, 11t www.sandatlas.org, 11m Artography, 11b Steinar, 13b Kilroy79, 14t Gyvafoto, 14m Bragin Alexey, 14b vilax, 15t Frontpage, 15m Tom Grundy, 15b serazetdinov, 16t www.sandatlas.org, 16b Gigi Peis, 17m Jurik Peter, 18t FeSeven, 18b Kletr, 19t www.sandatlas.org, 19m Bryan Busovicki, 20b Oliver Denker, 21b Oliver Denker, 23t Fokin Oleg, 23l NotionPic, 23r vavavka, 24m Sarah2, 24b sonsam, 25m Tyler Boyes, 25bl PocketsRockets; 25blm schankz; 25bm Jenny Zhang; 25brm Zinchenko Ivan; 25br Tiplyashina Evgeniya; 25br Andrii M, 26t vvoe, 26b Gaspar Janos, 27b Gaspar Janos, 28t Alexsandr Pobedimskiy, 28m Marisa Estivill, 28b Maciek67, 29m Olena Tur29b puttsk, 30t vvoe, 30b Sementer, 31t vvoe, 31m Natsmith1, 31b SHTRAUS DMYTRO, 32-33 Puslatronik, 34b Rattachon Angmanee, 39t Galina Barskaya, 39m gonetothemoon, 39b Alessandro Colle, 41t Moha El-Jaw; 41t Africa Studio; 41tm Bjoern Wylezich; 41m Viktor Kunz; 41m Albert Russ; 41m valzan; 41mb tanuha2001; 41mb bjphotographs; 41b STUDIO492; 41b Manutsawee Buapet, 42t STUDIO492, 42m Bjoern Wylezich, 43m vvoe, 43b vvoe, 44br Vector farther, 44bl Sean M Smith, 45tr Albert Russ, 45mr Kersti Lindstrom, 46r vvoe, 46l Albert Russ, 47t Albert Russ, 47b Albert Russ, 49t vvoe, 49b S_E, 50t Roy Palmer, 50m Alexander Sviridov, 52m Suponev Vladimir, 52b ZASIMOV YURII, 53t Albert Russ, 53b Albert Russ, 54t Sementer, 54b Albert Russ, 55t www.sandatlas.org, 55m MarcelClemens, 55b NatalieSchorr, 56b Sementer, 57t losmandarinas, 57m Versta, 57b Paulo Alfonso, 58t Mali lucky, 58b Albert Russ, 59t Albert Russ, 59b farbled, 60tm Armando Frazao, 60b John Le, 61m Dafinchi, 62t jmboix, 63tr Breck P. Kent, 63m vvoe, 63b Nyura, 64t farbled, 64b Roy Palmer, 65t Albert Russ, 65mr Zvonimir Atletic, 67t Cagla Acikgoz, 67m Moha El-Jaw, 68t vvoe, 69t Anastasia Bulanova, 71tr AlexussK, 71tl Albert Russ, 72l Hello RF Zcool, 72bl Roy Palmer, 73tl Albert Russ, 73tr Albert Russ, 73ml William G Forbes, 73mAlbert Russ, 73mr michal 812, 73lmr Branko Jovanovich, 74t Albert Russ, 74b Albert Russ, 75m vvoe, 75b Phil Degginger, 76m Mullek Josef, 76b RomanVX, 77t Dmitry Abezgauz, 77b vvoe, 78m Björn Wylezich, 78b Vereschagin, 79t Jiri Vaclavek, 79m Dafinchi, 79b MarcelClemens, 80b MarcelClemens, 81t Madlen, 81m photo-world, 82t arka38, 82-83 stihii, 83t Alex Coan, 84t Catmando, 85t Ariantolog, 85m arousa, 86t Warpaint, 86b Warpaint, 87t Warpaint, 89m tinkivinki, 89b Breck P. Kent, 90m AKKHARAT JARUSILAWONG, 90b Barks, 91t Linda Bucklin, 91m rehtse_c, 92t Linda Bucklin, 93t frantic00, 93m Michael Rosskothen, 93b Warpaint, 94b Sebastian Janicki, 95t Mark Brandon, 95b Roy Palmer, 96b farbled

WIKIPEDIA COMMONS: 5t Alexander Van Driessche/Wikipedia, 40 Alexander Van Driessche/Wikipedia Commons

33br Professor S.J. Mojzsis, University of Colorado

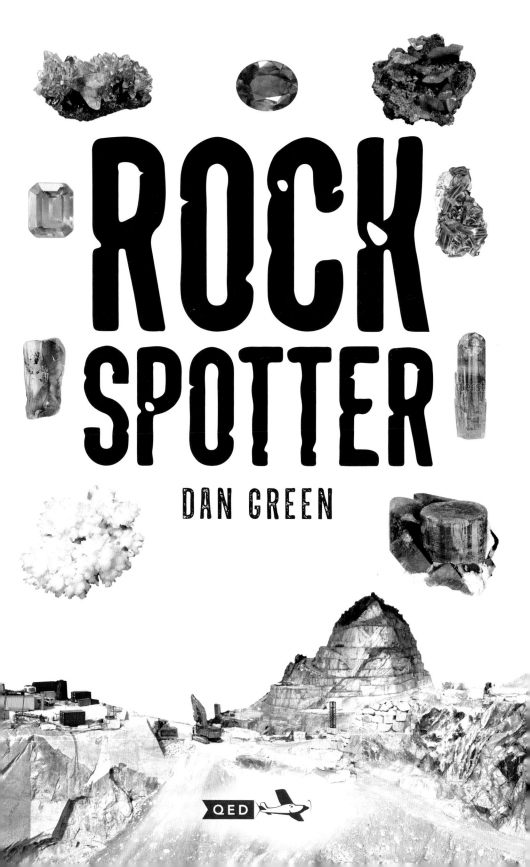

ROCK SPOTTER

DAN GREEN

CONTENTS

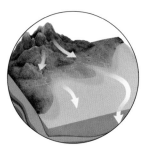

ROCK SPOTTER

Our rocky planet is full of natural wonders and marvels. This book will help you find these amazing rocks, minerals and fossils, and learn how to identify them.

ROCKS

We live on a rocky planet. Its surface has a hard topping of rocks that were melted and then cooled into solids, called igneous rocks. Along with these is a thin coating of sedimentary rocks. These are made of grains of older rocks, broken down by weathering and turned into sediment.

The final class are called metamorphic rocks. These formed when either igneous or sedimentary rocks changed deep within the Earth. This book will help you tell the difference between these three main groups and identify different examples from within the groups.

MINERALS

Every single rock is made of tiny chips of minerals. These are naturally occurring and form from the ingredients in the ground. They come in a huge range of colours and are shaped in regular, repeating patterns. In this book, you'll learn how to find out which group a mineral belongs to, and how to recognize some of the best-known mineral types.

FOSSILS

Buried in the rocks of Earth's crust are countless natural treasures. As well as gemstones, such as diamond and emerald, there are reminders of past ages on our planet. Many fossils are similar to plants and animals that are alive today. However, many more are life forms that are extinct and no longer exist on Earth. Learning about fossils tells us the way life began and how it has changed over 3.5 thousand million years.

WHAT YOU WILL NEED

You don't need any special equipment to go hunting for hidden treasures. The most important thing to take rock spotting is your eyes. Being a good rock spotter is all about seeing the tiny differences in rocks and minerals. With practice, you'll be able to pick out the twinkle of quartz (p70) or the colour of fluorite (p57).

Pack your rucksack with the following items:

- Hand lens or magnifying glass
- Rock hammer (ask an adult for help when using this)
- Safety glasses
- Spray bottle of water and brush
- Steel nail
- Notebook
- Labels and a pen, or a marker pen

And, of course... this book!
Have fun and enjoy rock spotting!

IGNEOUS ROCKS

Igneous rocks are made from melted rock. Many of them are dark coloured, but they often contain crystals that glitter and gleam when they catch the light.

Most of the time, the ground feels solid under our feet, but deep underground the Earth is warmer. As you go deeper it gets hot enough to melt rock. At temperatures around 1250 °C, the solid rock turns into a red-hot gloop called magma. The easiest-to-melt parts go first and, because they are lighter than the surrounding unmelted rock, they start to rise.

This magma collects in vast underground chambers and can force its way through the layers of the crust. It can even explode out onto the surface as lava. As the magma cools down, crystals form within it (p40), and it slowly hardens into a rock.

Types of igneous rock

There are two main types of igneous rock. **Intrusive igneous rock** (p10) forms when magma cools underground. **Volcanic igneous rock** (p16) forms when melted rocks hit the surface.

Fine grains form on the cool surface

Coarse grains form deeper inside the volcano

DID YOU KNOW?

For every kilometre you go underground, it gets 25 °C warmer. The Earth's core is even hotter than the Sun's outer layers!

HOW TO SPOT AN IGNEOUS ROCK

Igneous rocks are always made up of lots of crystals with flat faces and sharp edges. Sometimes these crystals are so tiny you need a magnifying glass to see them; but often they are much larger.

Although the crystals in igneous rocks seem all higgledy-piggledy, when you view them through a magnifying glass you will see they are interlocking. They share edges and often where one crystal ends, another has grown around it.

Fine-grained igneous rocks

Crystals take a long time to grow. When rocks have small crystals, this tells you that they cooled and formed very quickly.

Coarse-grained igneous rocks

Some igneous rocks have great big crystals. This tells the clued-up rock spotter that the rocks cooled slowly.

Different-sized crystal grains

Sometimes igneous rocks look like a chocolate-chip cookie, with large crystals embedded in a fine-grained rock. This happens when magma that has been cooling slowly underground is suddenly shot out onto the surface.

Rock-tionary

Magma (mag-ma) – hot, melted rock
Igneous (ig-nee-us) – this strange-sounding word means 'from fire'

INTRUSIVE ROCKS

Just as their pushy name suggests, intrusive igneous rocks forced their way up through and in between layers of solid rock. Formed by slow cooling, they all have medium- to large-grained interlocking crystals.

SYENITE

With its medium-sized crystals, syenite looks a bit like a light-coloured granite. The giveaway is that, unlike granite, syenite contains no quartz (p70). Instead, this rock has lots of creamy-white orthoclase feldspar (p68). Some syenites have shiny minerals that give the surface a shimmer when it catches the light.

SPOT IT

Syenite can be found in volcanic regions, especially those inland. It is often used in the flooring and exteriors of fancy buildings.

DID YOU KNOW?

Syenite is named after the town of Syene in ancient Egypt. Today, Syene is a city called Aswan, and is famous for its mighty dam.

DIORITE

Diorite is an easy one for rock spotters. It's called a 'salt and pepper' rock because of its black and white speckles. It has a similar make up of minerals to granite, but diorite's crystals are smaller. Potassium feldspar (p68) sometimes gives this igneous rock a pinkish colour.

SPOT IT

These are found in thin horizontal and vertical sheets of igneous rock between other rocks.

10

SPOT IT
This hard stone is used as 'fill' for roads and railway beds. It is sometimes used as 'black granite' facing for the outside of buildings.

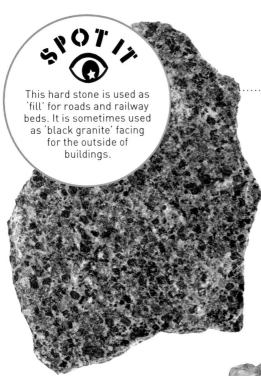

GABBRO

This important rock makes up a lot of the Earth's crust. It looks very much like a dark grey basalt (p16), but it has bigger crystals. Gabbro rocks often have lumps and bumps on their weathered surfaces.

ANORTHOSITE

This pinky-white igneous rock is unusual. Unlike most rocks, which are made of a mix of many minerals, anorthosite is almost entirely composed of one single mineral, plagioclase feldspar (p68). These ghostly white rocks form the highlands and pale areas of the Moon. A form of anorthosite, called spectrolite, shimmers under blue light.

DID YOU KNOW?
Intrusive rocks are sometimes called plutonic rocks. Pluto was the Roman god of the underworld.

INTRUSIVE ROCKS

These intrusive igneous rocks come from deep within the Earth's crust, so are rare on the surface. Some even formed in the Earth's mantle – the liquid layer underneath the crust.

PEGMATITE

The enormous crystals of pegmatite make it a very easy rock to identify – no other rock has such bumper crystals. As well as massive quartzes, pegmatite contains crystals of mica (p69), which can measure several metres across and can even contain gemstones, such as emeralds and tourmalines. This rock is also an important source of metal ores, such as lead, silver, tin and tungsten.

SPOT IT

Look for light veins in granite, with jumbo-sized crystals.

Rock-tionary

Ore – a rock or mineral containing valuable metals

PERIDOTITE

Peridotite is a dense, dark rock that is greenish-black in colour and feels heavy in the hand. The green colour in this rock is the mineral olivine (p75). The red parts are garnets. Peridotite's crystal grains are always large, because the rock forms in the Earth's upper mantle, 30–200 kilometres below the Earth's surface.

SPOT IT

Peridotite is found where the lava tubes of long-dead volcanoes are exposed, or slabs of ocean crust have been heaved up onto the land.

DUNITE

Fresh surfaces of dunite are a striking and attractive bright green – not many rocks are this colour. Dunite is almost entirely made up of the green mineral olivine. Exposed to the weather, however, dunite quickly dulls to a yellowish-green colour. This rock is a rare type of peridotite, and is an important source of the shiny metal chromium.

KIMBERLITE

Kimberlite is another variety of peridotite. With its dull, dark greenish-grey appearance, this rock doesn't look like it would contain hidden surprises. However, kimberlite is known for having large crystals, such as diamonds, and chunks of mantle rock embedded inside it.

Mirny Mine, Russia

SPOT IT

Kimberlite is found within the natural, carrot-shaped pipes that bring volcanic rocks up from deep within the Earth.

DID YOU KNOW?

Diamonds found in kimberlite formed 140–190 kilometres beneath the Earth's surface.

GRANITE

**Tough and durable, grim-faced granite will last forever.
This is the most common intrusive igneous rock on the planet.**

Nearly three-quarters of the land under your feet is made up of granite. If you look around, you may see many different types of rock on the Earth's surface, but if you dig down a little further, the chances are you'll find granite. The crust that makes up the continents can be up to 40 kilometres thick and its origins are mostly granite. In some places, the granite at the base of the continents is the remnants of Earth's very first crust.

Granite is another 'salt and pepper' rock, with flecks of white quartz and feldspar, mixed with black biotite mica. Overall, it is usually light-coloured, sometimes with a touch of pink which comes from orthoclase feldspar (p68).

Red granite rock with large quartz crystals

SPOT IT

Granite's interlocking crystals produce beautiful surfaces when polished. It comes in many colours, from black to red and green. You'll find it glinting on kitchen worktops, table tops and in the lobby areas of banks and hotels.

Granite crystals are generally large, due to the rock having cooled down slowly underground. A really large crystal will sometimes stick out from within the average-sized grains. These oddball crystals are called phenocrysts (say 'fee-no-krist') – they began growing earlier than the rest of the minerals.

Pink granite with large orthoclase crystals

DID YOU KNOW?

The boxer Floyd Mayweather used to boast of having a granite chin. He didn't mean that it was mottled and spotty, but that it was so hard his opponents would break their fists on it!

VOLCANIC ROCKS

There are about 1500 active volcanoes on land and perhaps as many as one million underwater. When they erupt, they pour molten lava over the Earth's surface at temperatures of 1200°C. This cools quickly to form fine-grained extrusive igneous rocks.

BASALT

Gloomy as a cloudy day, basalt gives nothing away. This is a dark grey-black stone that feels heavy in the hand. It is made up of crystal grains so tiny that you'll need a magnifying glass to see them. Despite its unfriendly outward appearance, basalt is the world's most common volcanic rock, forming most of the crust under the Earth's oceans.

DID YOU KNOW?

The dark patches on the Moon are basalt lava flows.

SPOT IT

Basalt columns can be seen at the Giant's Causeway in Northern Ireland. Cobblestones and road gravel are often made of this rock too.

ANDESITE

This rock may get its name from the Andes Mountains of South America, but just like basalt, andesite is everywhere! A fine-grained volcanic rock, its crystals are too small to see without a magnifying glass. However, the rock often contains larger grains within it, such as plagioclase, amphibole or pyroxene minerals. Andesite is generally light-coloured. It forms the heart of the famous Japanese volcano, Mount Fuji.

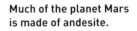

Much of the planet Mars is made of andesite.

RHYOLITE

Rhyolite is another light-coloured and fine-grained igneous rock. It contains lots of quartz and feldspar, and often has larger crystals embedded in a glassy, fine material. This results in small, rounded bobbles on the rock's surface, similar to syenite (p10). Rhyolite is light in the hand. As lava, it is sticky and erupts dangerously and explosively, so the rocks often show layering or banding like sedimentary rock.

SPOT IT

Rhyolites are relatively rare, but you may find this pinkish rock around lava domes inside active volcanoes, such as Mount St Helens in the United States.

17

VOLCANIC ROCKS

As well as free-flowing, sticky lava, volcanoes also produce a heap of unusual, freaky and downright weird rocks. Here are some of them.

PUMICE

A violent eruption of hot, sticky magma produces pumice, one of the strangest volcanic rocks. The lava, pumped full of dissolved gases, foams like a bottle of fizzy pop that has been shaken up. It hardens quickly, but the glassy rock is left full of bubbles and air pockets like an aerated chocolate bar. Pumice is usually white, cream or light grey in colour, but can also be bluish, green-brown or black.

DID YOU KNOW?

Pumice is so full of bubbles that it floats on water!

SPOT IT

You might find this frothy rock in the bathroom, where it's often used as a foot scrubber.

OBSIDIAN

Obsidian is a volcanic rock that has cooled too quickly to form any crystals. Instead, it's a glassy lump with a shiny, mirror-like surface. Obsidian is almost always jet black but it can be red if it contains the iron-rich mineral haematite.

SPOT IT

This rock is still used for razor-sharp surgical blades. Look for rounded pebbles of obsidian, often called 'Apache tears'.

TUFF

Tuff is solidified volcanic ash. Most volcanoes produce ash when the enormous pressures of an eruption blast magma apart into a trillion tiny pieces. The ash collects in thick beds, like a sedimentary rock. This light-coloured, soft stone is sometimes layered like sandstone, and can have fragments of pumice inside it. Welded tuff occurs when the ash is hot enough to join particles together.

SPOT IT

Tuff is most often found near the sites of ancient volcanoes. Look for bedding layers, like sedimentary rocks. The famous moai rock statues on Easter Island are carved from tuff.

ROCK SPOTTING TIP

Don't confuse tuff with tufa (p30). Tufa is a limestone, which often contains shells and fossils.

PELE'S HAIR

This odd rock forms when erupting molten lava is spun out into long, hairlike strands by the wind. Named after the Hawaiian goddess of fire, the wispy mineral fibres are light enough to be carried off by a gust of air.

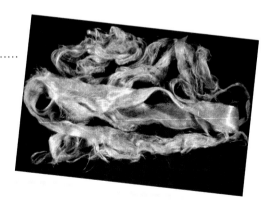

ROCKS FROM SPACE

As our planet speeds through space, it is constantly peppered with space rocks or meteorites. Some of the rocks that fall from the sky are the oldest ever found. There are three types of meteorite.

STONY METEORITES

Nearly all of the rocks that fall to Earth are stony meteorites. They once belonged to a planet or asteroid. They look and feel much like ordinary Earth rocks, but sometimes have a telltale blackened outer crust, caused by scorching as they blazed through the Earth's atmosphere. Inside almost every stony meteorite are mysterious round grains, which come from a time before the planets formed, 4.5 billion years ago.

A fragment of the Chelyabinsk meteorite that fell in Russia, in 2013.

SPOT IT

The best places to look for stony meteorites are in Antarctica and the deserts of Saudi Arabia.

DID YOU KNOW?

What's the difference between meteors and meteorites? Planet Earth often collides with tiny dust-sized particles. As they burn up in the atmosphere, these meteors create a streak of light called a shooting star. Larger chunks of rock make it to the ground without being destroyed. These are then known as meteorites and can punch massive craters in the Earth's surface on impact.

IRON METEORITES

These were once the central cores of long-gone planets or large asteroids. Iron meteorites often have exotic and spectacular shapes, which have been forged by heat on their journey to the Earth's surface. Since these meteorites are 90–95 per cent iron (along with nickel), they feel much heavier than most rock.

DID YOU KNOW?

Sometimes meteorites come from the Moon or Mars, and land on Earth. They are extremely rare. Of over 61,000 space rocks found, only around 130 have come from Mars.

Try barren places where dark meteorites stick out against the background. You can also search for iron meteorites with a metal detector.

STONY-IRON METEORITES

The stony-irons are the rarest of all three types of meteorite. These visitors from outer space have roughly equal amounts of nickel-iron and stone.

Find a place where a meteorite has fallen and look for small chunks and fragments that have broken off the main rock.

SEDIMENTARY ROCKS

Sedimentary rocks are recycled rocks. Created by the movement of water over the Earth's surface, they are made up of grains worn off older rocks.

Rocks on the Earth's surface take a beating. They are lashed by rain, prised apart by plant roots, attacked by chemicals and shattered by frosts. As they wear down, the broken fragments slip down slopes or are carried off by rivers, and even glaciers, towards the sea.

These grains of eroded rock are what turn rivers brown – they are called sediments. Scoop up a glass of river water and you'll see it become clear as the sediment settles to the bottom. Once a river no longer has the energy to transport it, sediment is dumped. The grains collect on riverbeds and beaches. Over time, sediments are buried under fresh deposits and are slowly squeezed to become solid rock.

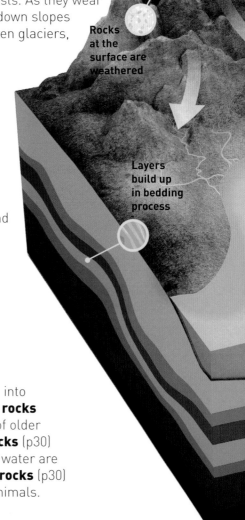

Rocks at the surface are weathered

Layers build up in bedding process

Types of sedimentary rock

Sedimentary rocks can be divided into three types. **Clastic sedimentary rocks** (p24) are made from broken bits of older rocks. **Chemical sedimentary rocks** (p30) form when materials dissolved in water are deposited. **Organic sedimentary rocks** (p30) are made from bits of plants or animals.

HOW TO SPOT A SEDIMENTARY ROCK

 Bedding

Sediments are deposited, one type on top of the last. This means they mostly build up in flat layers. This 'bedding' process shows up in sedimentary rocks, making them look like the pages of a book.

Grains

Most sedimentary rocks have grains. Unlike igneous rocks, with their interlocking crystals, the particles in a sedimentary rock do not mesh with each other. Grains in sedimentary rock can be the size of large pebbles or cobblestones, or tiny particles of mud, silt or grit.

As the grains travel, they bash and grind, getting their sharp edges knocked off. This makes grains smaller and more rounded the further they have travelled.

Sediments also get sorted by size as a river's energy decreases. The heavier grains get dumped, but the lightest grains travel further.

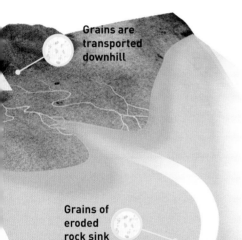

Grains are transported downhill

Grains of eroded rock sink

New grains press down on older layers

DID YOU KNOW?

Sedimentary rocks cover nearly the entire surface of the planet. This is only a very thin coating, however, so they are not a significant part of Earth's crust.

CLASTIC ROCKS

Sedimentary rocks contain grains that range from fine particles of silt and clay, to pebbles and boulders. The larger the grains, the shorter the distance a sediment has travelled from its parent rock.

MUDSTONE

Mudstone is made of tiny clay particles that can only be seen with a magnifying glass. It is deposited in quiet, low-energy parts of a river. Mud builds up in thick gloopy layers on tidal flats, the seabed and lakebeds. Since it is made of the finest sediment, mudstone is flat and dull-coloured, and preserves fossils well.

SPOT IT

Look for shale in scree slopes at the base of cliffs, but beware of falling rocks! Some shale may contain fossils.

SHALE

Shale is a dark grey to black, flaky stone. Closely related to mudstone, shale forms when mudstone gets squashed down, deep inside the Earth. It splits easily into thin flakes. Where this rock is sticking out from a cliff, there is often a scree slope at the base.

DID YOU KNOW?

Shale is a very common rock on Mars.

CONGLOMERATE

Lumpy, bumpy conglomerates look like a pudding that's gone solid. They are made of rounded pebbles or cobblestones cemented together. With the biggest grains of all sedimentary rocks, there's no mistaking them. Conglomerates are the kind of rock formed on a pebble or storm beach.

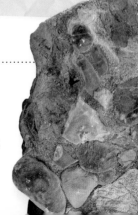

GRITSTONE

As its name suggests, gritstone has coarse grains that are larger than sand. Gritstone feels rough and scratchy to touch. Climbers love it because it's so easy to grip on to. Gritstone is so tough, it was once used to make millstones for grinding grain, and grindstones to sharpen blades.

SPOT IT

You may see abandoned round millstones dotting the countryside, in areas where they were once used.

BRECCIA

Like conglomerates, breccia contains large rock fragments. However, instead of being smooth and rounded, breccia is angular. This is because the grains have not been transported far. Breccia contains both large and small grains. This is the sort of deposit left by a glacier or formed by a scree slope.

ROCK SPOTTING TIP

Breccias are often found along faults in rocks, where one block of rock has thrust past another. When solid rock rubs together, the rocks in the middle get mashed and shattered.

NAME THAT SEDIMENT!

Scoop up a cup of river water in a clear container. Put the container on a flat surface and wait a few minutes for the sediments to settle. Can you categorise them all? You'll need a magnifying glass to see the grains in the muds and silts.

Mud	Silt	Sand	Gravel	Cobble	Boulder
<0.002 mm	0.002–0.06 mm	0.06–2 mm	2–60 mm	60–200 mm	>200 mm

CLASTIC ROCKS

As well as sandy rocks containing quartz grains, clastic sedimentary rocks can also be composed of other minerals. This group of rocks are made of grains of a hard but soluble mineral, called calcium carbonate. Calcium carbonate is a common mineral, which sea creatures use to build their shells.

GREYWACKE

Sometimes called 'dirty sandstone', greywacke is hard rock made up of quartz grains, mixed with silt and mud. Formed by underwater avalanches, greywacke is a light to darkish grey rock and is often shot through with bright white veins of quartz. It can sometimes contain calcium carbonate and often looks like basalt.

SPOT IT
Many beaches are made of rounded pebbles of light grey-coloured greywacke.

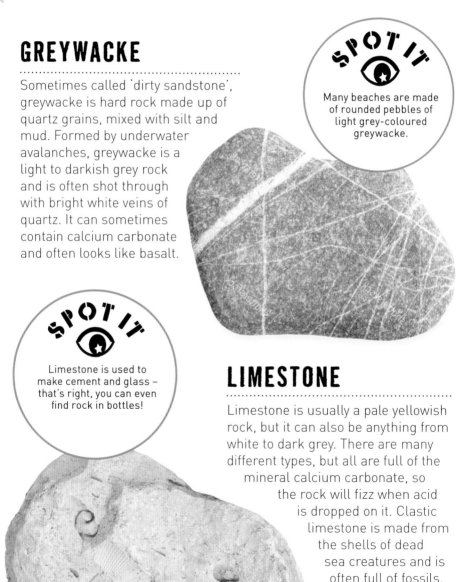

SPOT IT
Limestone is used to make cement and glass – that's right, you can even find rock in bottles!

LIMESTONE

Limestone is usually a pale yellowish rock, but it can also be anything from white to dark grey. There are many different types, but all are full of the mineral calcium carbonate, so the rock will fizz when acid is dropped on it. Clastic limestone is made from the shells of dead sea creatures and is often full of fossils.

CHALK

Chalk is a form of limestone made from the shells of microscopic sea life. It is a soft white or greyish rock with a powdery texture, and often contains rounded nodules of flint. Although the individual shells are incredibly small, so many are laid down that a thick layer is created. Chalk that was deposited during the age of dinosaurs makes up the vast white cliffs seen in the south of England, north of France and Denmark.

SPOT IT

You can find this rock ground up in putty, paint and even food.

DOLOMITE

Confusingly, dolomite is both the name of a rock and a common mineral. Sometimes called dolostone for this reason, dolomite is a hard, compact rock. Pale coloured in whites or light pinks and greys, its surfaces have a sugary sparkle. Containing carbonate minerals, dolomite fizzes on contact with acid.

SPOT IT

The craggy Dolomite Mountains of northern Italy are made of this rock.

SANDSTONE

Sandstone is a rock that makes you think of beaches, dunes, deserts and summer sun. This golden-coloured rock is made from small grains of sand.

Sandstone is one of the most common sedimentary rocks on Earth. It is made from sand-sized chips of quartz (p70), laid down in layers. Sandstone has many colours, from green to chocolate-brown, but the standard stone is a warm yellow or tan colour.

Sand, silt and gravel laid down millions of years ago by ancient rivers have become the colourful hills of the Blue Mesa in Arizona, USA.

Sand gets everywhere – as you will know if you've ever been to the beach! Grains of sand are between 0.06 mm and 0.2 mm across, and since the quartz it is made from is super hardwearing, sand is found in many environments. Sand gets deposited on riverbanks, lakebeds and marine shorelines, as well as in dry deserts.

Sandstone sculptures stand the test of time. This statue of Egyptian pharaoh Akhenaten is over 3000 years old.

The size of the grains in sandstone tells keen rock spotters how the sediment was transported and deposited. Wind-blown sand is extremely fine, whereas beach deposits may be coarse and mixed up with silt and mud. Sandstone may also contain feldspar minerals (p68), and sometimes mica and olivine. The cement that glues the grains together gives the rock its colour. Calcium carbonate cement makes a tan or yellow stone; iron oxide cement is brown; and rarer manganese compounds give the rock a purplish colour.

Due to the toughness of its grains, sandstone is durable. However, it is relatively easy to cut and shape. Block-shaped sandstones, in tan, brown and honey colours, are commonly used for building and paving, and it is also often used for ornamental sculptures.

Classic honey-coloured sandstone was used to build the memorial tombs of the Royal Cenotaphs in India.

ROCK SPOTTING TIP

Sand in motion creates interesting patterns in rock. Ripple marks created by water currents, or the passage of the tides across a beach, are often clearly visible on exposed sandstone surfaces. Sand is not always deposited on flat surfaces, either. The steep sides of desert sand dunes create sweeping patterns on rock outcrops, called cross-bedding.

The world-famous 'wave' of Coyote Butte North in Utah and Arizona, USA, is formed of sandstone beds laid down over millions of years.

CHEMICAL AND ORGANIC ROCKS

Chemical sedimentary rocks form when minerals dissolved in water are deposited as solid grains. Organic sediments are produced from organic matter such as plants or animals.

TUFA

Not to be confused with tuff (p19), tufa is an unusual looking, soft limestone. It forms in mineral springs where the water contains lots of dissolved calcium carbonate. The mineral is deposited in crazy shapes, sometimes in tall towers that reach 10 metres out of the water. Travertine is another form of limestone deposited by hot springs. Both rocks are cream or tan-coloured.

Rock-tionary

Precipitate (pre-si-pi-tate) – when a solid substance is deposited out of a liquid solution

SPOT IT

You can find tufa forming in salt pans and low-lying lakes in hot regions. Travertine is often used for tiles in bathrooms.

OOLITIC LIMESTONE

Oolite or 'egg stone' is an odd limestone composed of tiny balls of calcium carbonate. The spheres are 0.25–2 millimetres across and give the rock a bobbly surface, a bit like gritstone. They form when calcium carbonate is precipitated in flowing water that keeps the grains rolling and tumbling. Limestone containing pea-sized balls is known as pisolite.

SEDIMENTARY

FLINT

Flint, or chert, is an extremely hard rock that occurs in rounded lumps inside chalk and marine limestone. The nodules are brown or grey inside, with a rough white crust. Flint is made of quartz crystals that are so small you won't be able to see them, even with a magnifying glass.

The 'clinker' beaches of southeast England are made of hardwearing flint pebbles.

DID YOU KNOW?

When flint breaks it leaves a sharp edge. Stone Age people used flint to make knives, axes and arrowheads.

COAL

Coal is a brownish-black rock made from the remains of dead plants. Occurring as a soft, loose, brown stone (lignite) or a shiny, dense, jet-black rock (anthracite), coal was formed in ancient tropical swamplands. It is now found in layers or veins, called coal beds, and is dug out of the ground to use as a fuel to generate electricity. Burning coal releases carbon dioxide into the atmosphere, which is a cause of global warming.

METAMORPHIC ROCKS

Metamorphic rocks are shapeshifters. Rocks change their character when they are heated and squeezed deep inside the Earth, and an entirely new rock is born.

Our planet is not the quiet place it might appear. Unbelievably, vast slabs of rock carrying entire continents trundle across the surface, driven by the heat energy inside the Earth. These tectonic plates are constantly on the move, and they bump and collide with each other. Deep underground, rocks are squeezed as if trapped in a gigantic vice, and stewed under enormous pressures and temperatures. Put through this kind of punishment, they begin to change.

Metamorphic rocks form when pre-existing rocks are transformed underground. The changes alter both the rock's texture and its minerals. Crushing and heating force different minerals to crystallize. Grains change shape and interlock, filling gaps and holes. Minerals, such as quartz, migrate to form veins within the rock. At maximum mangling, the rock is completely recast and its original sedimentary and igneous features are wiped clean.

Nothing escapes metamorphism. All rocks eventually change their character, and the oldest ones on the planet are all metamorphic rocks.

Pressure from surface rocks

Heat from magma

Metamorphic rock forming

Magma

Types of metamorphic rock

There are two main types of metamorphic rock – those with layers or bands, called **foliated** (p34), and those without, called **non-foliated** (p36). Most metamorphic rocks are created by a combination of pressure and heat. Pressure tends to create foliated textures and heat results in non-foliated metamorphics.

HOW TO SPOT A METAMORPHIC ROCK

 No layers

Metamorphic rocks without layers have no horizontal or parallel features. They can only be identified by the minerals they contain.

Layers

Layering in metamorphic rocks happens when pressure forces certain minerals to line up in the same direction. This produces parallel, flat surfaces, as in slate, or more extreme wavy forms with larger crystals, such as schist. The easiest to recognize is banding, seen in the alternating dark and light bands of gneiss.

DID YOU KNOW?

The oldest rocks on Earth are in Canada. The Acasta Gneiss (below) is dated at 4.03 billion years old.

BANDED ROCKS

As the surface of the planet shifts and buckles, pressure builds up in the rocks of the crust. The pressure pushes minerals about within the rock, forcing them to change direction and line up. The more intense the pressure, the more extreme the changes. The minerals slowly arrange themselves into striped bands or thin sheets, like a stack of paper.

SLATE

This dull looking rock is dark grey to black, sometimes with a tinge of purple. Slate forms from sedimentary shale or mudstone. Under pressure, minerals in the rock realign. They stack up in sheets, like the pages of a book. This means that slate splits easily into thin, flat slabs. Slate often contains great fossils.

SPOT IT

Look for roofs with slate tiles. Slate was also used for traditional chalk boards in schools and can still be found on super-flat pro snooker tables.

SCHIST

This is a rock with lots of sparkle! Look closely and you'll see that many of its mineral grains lie parallel to each other, stretched out in one direction. The rock also has clear bands. A mica schist contains lots of thin, flaky crystals of mica (p68), which give it a shiny, sequined appearance.

MYLONITE

Mylonite looks like it has been squeezed out of a tube of toothpaste. This stone forms deep underground, where intense temperatures and pressures turn rocks to putty. The squeezing forces flatten the minerals, leaving mylonite with squished crystals, called porphyroclasts, embedded in a fine-grained streaky rock.

SPOT IT

Gravel and crushed stones of mylonite are used for construction and road building.

Rock-tionary

Porphyroclast (poor-fyre-oh-clast) – fragments of older crystals embedded in rock of newer, finer grains

GNEISS

This rock is pronounced 'nice', and very nice it is too! Gneiss is an exceptionally hard rock with large grains in thin, dark and light bands. It forms deep below mountain ranges. The lighter bands usually contain lots of quartz (p70) and feldspar (p69), whereas the dark minerals are hornblende (p73) and biotite mica (p68).

ROCK SPOTTING TIP

Sometimes gneiss has crazy, wavy bands running through it, which look just like granite. This happens when the rock has become so mangled that parts of it have melted completely. This type of rock is called a migmatite.

NON-BANDED ROCKS

Not all metamorphic rocks are banded or pressed into sheetlike layers. Rocks that have been altered by heat as much as pressure, tend to be solid with grainy textures.

METAMORPHIC

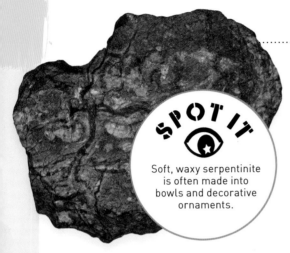

SERPENTINITE

As its name suggest, this greenish rock looks a little like snakeskin. Soft and oily to the touch, it contains lots of the mineral serpentine. This metamorphic rock forms deep beneath the ocean floor, where hot water is forced through mantle rocks. There may be lots of it underground, but it is rare to find it on the surface.

SPOT IT

Soft, waxy serpentinite is often made into bowls and decorative ornaments.

ROCK SPOTTING TIP

Serpentinite often contains very thin strands of the mineral chrysotile. These strands are light enough to float in the air and are damaging to the lungs if inhaled. They were used to make a material known as asbestos. Until we realised how harmful it was, asbestos was used in building insulation.

HORNFELS

This is another rock that confusingly has the same name as a mineral. Hornfels is a dark to black, moody looking, fine-grained stone. Typically, it is found bordering igneous rock, where hot magma has pushed its way into cracks from under the surface. The rock surrounding these cracks is baked hard, turning into hornfels.

SPOT IT

This hard rock is often used for gravel in construction.

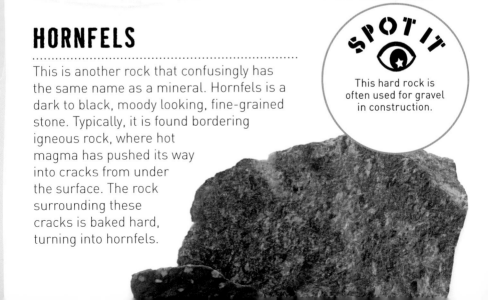

QUARTZITE

Tougher than tough, this metamorphic marvel is formed when sandstone is baked hard under the surface. The sand grains of the original rock recrystallize to form interlocking grains with no gaps in between. In a similar process to the formation of marble, the large, irregularly shaped crystals give the rock a sugary appearance.

AMPHIBOLITE

Showing no banding at all, amphibolite is a coarse-grained metamorphic rock. Although it contains very little quartz, amphibolite can look a bit like igneous diorite or granite. The rock is mainly made of amphibole minerals, such as hornblende (p73) and plagioclase (p68). It can be black or dark green, depending on the type of mineral it contains.

FULGURITE

Sometimes called fossilized lightning, fulgurites are knobbly hollow tubes of glassy stone, made when lightning strikes sand. The intense temperature fuses the grains of sand together.

DID YOU KNOW?

These fused sand tubes are rare. The longest ever found measured 30 metres – as long as six buses!

DID YOU KNOW?

The core of a lightning strike is an incredible 50,000 °C. That's nearly ten times hotter than the surface of the Sun and way past the melting point of sand (1700 °C).

METAMORPHIC

MARBLE

Marble is a beautiful metamorphic rock which comes in many colours. This tough, good-looking rock is made when limestone is buried deep within the crust, where heat and pressure cause changes.

This famous material forms when carbonate rocks, such as limestone and dolomite, are squeezed and heated under the Earth. The intense heat and pressure are enough to make crystals of calcium carbonate recrystallize. The mineral grains interlock with each other, creating marble's well-known sugary texture.

Also known as onion stone, Cipollino marble comes from quarries in Greece.

METAMORPHIC

Marble has odd-shaped grains. Locking together, they give the rock its colour and smoothness when polished. Instead of a clear, glassy reflection, light is scattered off its surface, gracing the stone with a soft glow. The most common colour of marble is an off-white, but impurities make it colourful. There are over 3000 different types of marble, including green, blue and even black and gold varieties.

Marble is mainly made of white calcite, but other minerals, such as serpentine, give it different colours.

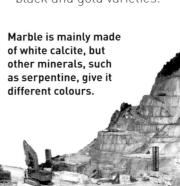

Soft enough to carve, yet hard enough to hold a polish and resist scratches, marble can be found in the receptions of swanky buildings. Some of the world's most famous statues are carved in marble. Michelangelo's works of art are carved in flawless, white Carrara marble.

Many famous sculptors have worked with marble. This ancient Greek sculpture is called the Venus de Milo.

Marble is harder than limestone and has larger grains. Fossils may sometimes be found in marble, but small ones are usually wiped out. As marble is a carbonate rock, it fizzes when acid is dropped upon it. This means that marble sculptures and buildings are slowly eaten away by slightly acidic rainwater.

DID YOU KNOW?

Ashgabat in Turkmenistan, also known as the 'City of White Marble', is renowned as having the most marble buildings in the world. The white marble lining its 543 new buildings covers a total area of 4.5 million square metres!

METAMORPHIC

Some of the most famous marbles come from the quarries of Carrara, Italy.

MINERALS

Rocks are made up of millions of tiny grains. These naturally occurring grains are minerals. Most minerals are small, but they can sometimes grow to surprisingly large sizes.

What is a mineral?

If you look at most rocks through a magnifying glass, you will see lots of tiny crystals glinting on the surface. Although they are entirely natural, they are not living things. They grow as liquids and harden into solids, forming shapes with regular, repeating patterns. Each different shape and colour belongs to a different mineral; each mineral has different chemical ingredients.

DID YOU KNOW?

The world's largest minerals are found in Mexico's Cave of Crystals. The giant gypsum crystals are over 10 metres long – that's longer than a bus!

ROCK SPOTTING TIP

Pick up a solid object from the ground.
Take a good look at it. How can you tell if it is a mineral?

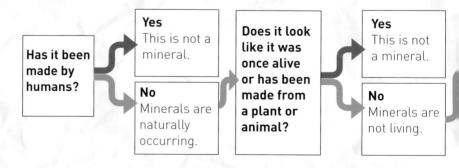

Has it been made by humans?

Yes
This is not a mineral.

No
Minerals are naturally occurring.

Does it look like it was once alive or has been made from a plant or animal?

Yes
This is not a mineral.

No
Minerals are not living.

Sometimes you need a microscope to see the crystals in minerals, so use the images in this book to help you identify minerals if you are unsure.

DID YOU KNOW?

There are more than 4000 types of mineral, but only about 100 of them are commonly found on the Earth's surface.

Mohs scale

Once you've found a mineral, a great way of identifying it is to test its hardness. Each mineral is ranked between 1 and 10 on the Mohs scale, where 1 is the softest and 10 is the hardest. Since harder solids will scratch the surfaces of softer solids, you can tell where a mineral lies on the scale by testing it against materials you know.

Does it have crystals?

Yes
It's a mineral! Minerals are naturally occurring solids, with a definite mix of chemicals. Due to these chemical ingredients and the arrangement of atoms, minerals grow as crystals.

No
Check again with a magnifying glass as the crystals may not be easy to see.

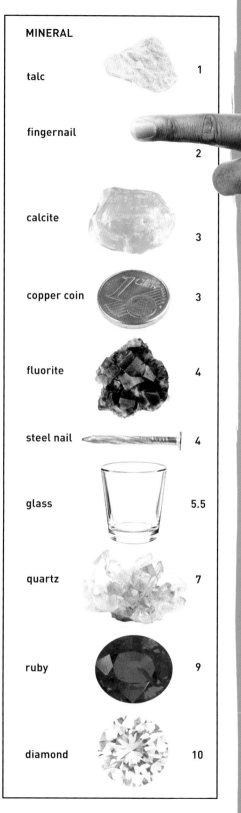

MINERAL	
talc	1
fingernail	2
calcite	3
copper coin	3
fluorite	4
steel nail	4
glass	5.5
quartz	7
ruby	9
diamond	10

NATIVE MINERALS

Native minerals occur in nature in their pure form, uncombined with other substances. This stable and unreactive group includes some precious metals and valuable non-metals.

SILVER

Found unaltered in Earth's crust, silver has been mined since ancient times. In legends, this pale and shiny precious metal is said to kill werewolves. One of the strangest forms of native silver – called dendritic silver – looks like a crazy mass of fingers and twisted wires.

SPOT IT
You're more likely to find silver in jewellery and coins than in werewolf-slaying silver bullets!

SPOT IT
Look for copper water pipes in your home.

COPPER

This important metal is rarely found in its native state. There's much more copper in ore minerals, such as chalcopyrite and cuprite. When it is found in its pure form, this red-brown metal often forms huge crystals. The largest crystal ever found weighed 420 tonnes!

DID YOU KNOW?

Money is useless if the materials in the coins are worth more than the face value itself. For this reason you won't find much copper in modern coins. Since 1992, UK pennies have been made of copper-plated steel.

DIAMOND

Shining bright, there's no mistaking this expensive gem. Diamonds may be called 'rocks', but they are definitely minerals. This crystal is a kind of pure carbon, formed deep underground. It is the hardest naturally occurring substance – so hard that drills tipped with diamond can cut straight through solid rock.

DID YOU KNOW?

Some diamonds are as ancient as a billion years old.

GRAPHITE

Just like diamond, graphite is made of pure carbon, but the difference is obvious. This big softie is one of the softest minerals on Earth. Instead of a clear, brilliant shining gemstone, graphite is a dull black or grey substance. It is mostly found in shapeless lumps that are soft and greasy to touch. Graphite is so soft it even leaves marks on paper.

SPOT IT

Find graphite mixed with clay inside pencil leads.

SULPHUR

Bright, canary-yellow sulphur has to be one of the easiest minerals to spot. Its buttery looking crystals are mainly found on the brims of smelly, gassy vents in volcanic areas or hot springs.

MINERALS

GOLD

This native mineral is a real winner. With its unusual colour and a shine that never fades, gold is one of the most precious metals on Earth.

Gold looks pretty and is extremely rare, which keeps its value high and means it is always in demand. Gold does not rust, tarnish or corrode. In fact, it is so chemically unreactive, it is almost always found as a pure metal and keeps its soft yellow sheen forever. The golden burial mask of the Egyptian pharaoh Tutankhamun has remained shiny for over 3000 years.

DID YOU KNOW?

99 per cent of all the gold on Earth is buried forever in the planet's core.

SPOT IT

Gold is used to make jewellery, coins and medals. You can find gold in electronic devices such as smartphones, where its ability to conduct electricity makes it very useful. You can even eat it – gold foil is used to decorate expensive chocolates. But don't eat your smartphone!

DID YOU KNOW?

A tonne of smartphones contains more gold than a tonne of gold ore.

DID YOU KNOW?

Gold is so soft and pliable it can be hammered until it's thin enough for light to shine through!

Gold can be found on an astronaut's helmet visor.

Although some lucky folk find nuggets of pure gold, most gold occurs as flakes or grains within an ore rock. Gold is heavy stuff: when it gets eroded out of rocks, it settles in river silt. This is why some of the best places to hunt for the precious metal are in sandbanks and riverbeds. Tiny gold flakes can be separated from mud by 'panning' – washing river silt through a sieve.

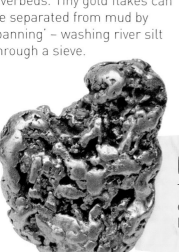

DID YOU KNOW?

The largest gold nugget ever found contained 71 kilograms of pure gold. It was named 'Welcome Stranger'.

MINERALS

Rock-tionary

Nugget (nuh-get) – (as in chicken or gold). A solid lump of something good! Although they are often very small, gold nuggets are a high-purity metal.

SULPHIDE MINERALS

This group of minerals is formed from a combination of sulphur plus one or more metallic elements. This makes sulphide minerals important sources of many metals for us to mine. Most sulphide minerals are soft, often dull and dark-coloured, and feel quite heavy.

GALENA

Galena is unmistakable, forming well-defined, dark, eight-sided crystals, with a wicked looking metallic gleam. Galena is the main ore of lead and is often found alongside other sulphide minerals in the veins of igneous and metamorphic rocks, such as marble. The mineral contains a whopping 86.6 per cent lead.

DID YOU KNOW?

The largest galena crystal ever found was a 25-centimetre cube in the Great Laxey Mine on the Isle of Man, UK.

SPOT IT

Galena is mined for the lead metal it contains. The number one use for lead is in car batteries.

CHALCOPYRITE

Found alongside pyrite in the veins of igneous rocks, this is probably the most commercially valuable sulphide mineral. Made of copper, iron and sulphur, vast quantities of this rock are mined to extract the useful metals. Rocks containing chalcopyrite are often dark, but the mineral itself is a dull brassy yellow. It is usually found in lumps, where the individual crystals are too small to see.

ROCK SPOTTING TIP

Scratch chalcopyrite against a rough surface. Although the mineral is yellow, its colour when powdered is a greenish-black.

SPHALERITE

Sphalerite is also called 'black jack' – it has a tricksy habit of fooling miners because it looks a lot like galena. Sphalerite is the most common ore of the metal zinc. Like many sulphides, it is often found alongside other minerals in the group, such as pyrite and chalcopyrite.

STIBNITE

Stibnite is the main ore of a soft metal called antimony. Crystals of stibnite can be absolutely stunning, with long, sharp needles that shine darkly like steel. They are often found in veins in granite rocks, along with other sulphide minerals, such as pyrite, galena, orpiment, realgar and cinnabar.

SPOT IT

You can find stibnite on the heads of safety matches. It is also an ingredient of flash powders, used for on-stage pyrotechnics.

SULPHIDE MINERALS

Not all sulphide minerals are dark and shiny. A few have vivid colours, and some even form glassy looking crystals. However, these minerals do not make good gemstones as they are too soft and easily chipped.

PYRITE

This mineral joker is famous for looking just like gold at first glance. There are no riches here though, just iron and sulphur. 'Fool's gold' grows in sharp-edged little cubes. It is the most common sulphide mineral in the planet's crust. Its bright, brassy colour also earns it the name 'brazzle'.

SPOT IT

Pyrite is easy to find in sedimentary, igneous and metamorphic rocks, appearing in veins of quartz. Deep underground, pyrite sometimes replaces the minerals in fossil bones and shells. You may discover these fossils with a beautiful, natural coat of gleaming gold.

ROCK SPOTTING TIP

Don't get dazzled by brazzle – learn to tell fool's gold apart from real gold. It's simple when you know how! Pyrite forms straight-edged cubes – something you won't see in gold. It's also hard, not soft like the precious metal; you'll need a steel nail to scratch pyrite. Pound it into a powder and, weirdly, the mineral smells fishy! If you scrape it down a rough surface the gold colour turns to a mucky greenish-black streak.

SPOT IT

You can discover realgar around volcanoes and hot springs.

REALGAR

This royal red mineral is also called 'ruby sulphur' and is soft and greasy. It is often found as lumps of tiny crystals, together with orpiment. These 'fire and brimstone' mineral twins both contain toxic arsenic.

SPOT IT

Orpiment forms a powdery crusting around volcanic vents and hot springs.

ORPIMENT

Related to realgar, this mineral's lurid orange-gold colour says 'don't touch'! Orpiment contains the toxic metal arsenic. Despite being poisonous, it was once used by artists in a paint called 'king's yellow'.

CINNABAR

Cinnabar is a bright red mineral and is the main ore of the liquid metal mercury. Rocks containing cinnabar sometimes 'sweat out' a bead of mercury, which lies shimmering on the surface.

SPOT IT

This mineral is found in grainy lumps – alongside stibnite and pyrite – in the veins of volcanic rocks. Very rarely, it forms brilliant scarlet crystals.

DID YOU KNOW?

Victorious Roman generals returning from war covered themselves in cinnabar and paraded in front of the emperor.

MINERALS

OXIDE MINERALS

The oxides are a fine-looking bunch of minerals. They are formed from a combination of oxygen and a variety of metals. Just like the sulphide minerals, they are important metal ores.

MAGNETITE

Magnetite is the most magnetic of all minerals. Too much magnetite around will make a compass go berserk! Many birds' beaks contain small crystals of magnetite, which may help them navigate using the Earth's magnetic field. Along with haematite, magnetite is an important ore of iron. Its eight-sided crystals look dark with a brownish tint and a glossy metallic sheen.

DID YOU KNOW?

Chitons, a type of mollusc that scrape algae off rocks, have tongues covered in tiny magnetite 'teeth'.

HAEMATITE

With an iron content that sometimes tops 70 per cent, this is one of the most important minerals in the world. Iron is the number one go-to engineering material, thanks to its strength, availability on the planet and cheapness to produce. Haematite has many different forms – two of the most common are glistening black, metallic, six-sided crystals, or smooth bean-shaped lumps with a reddish tinge. When you scratch haematite, its powder shows a blood-red streak.

DID YOU KNOW?

Haematite gets its name from the Greek word 'haima', meaning blood.

CHROMITE

Chromite may not be very exciting to look at but, as the only ore of shiny chromium metal, it is a very important mineral. Chromite is dull grey, usually lumpy looking and often has a slight metallic sheen to its surface.

Look for this mineral in metamorphic rocks that have been greatly changed by heat and pressure. You'll find it alongside minerals such as serpentinite.

Chromite in serpentinite rock

ROCK SPOTTING TIP

So you think you've found some chromite? Scratch the mineral firmly on a rough surface. If it's chromite, the powdered mineral will have a characteristic brown colour.

URANINITE

Also known as pitchblende, this mineral has opaque steel-black to brownish-black crystals, with a metallic or greasy gleam to them. They feel heavy because this mineral is rich in uranium, a radioactive metal used for fuel in nuclear power stations.

Look for black to steel-black patches, with tints of brown. Uraninite often looks bobbly, like the surface of a bunch of grapes. Rocks containing the mineral will feel surprisingly heavy in the hand.

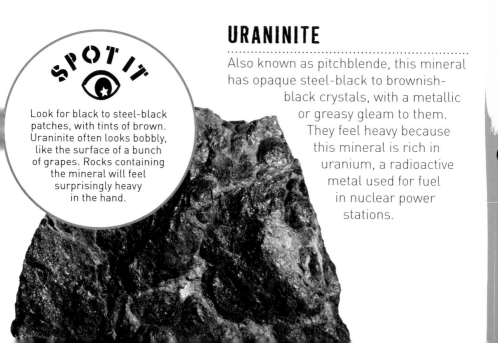

OXIDE MINERALS

As well as being important sources of metal, many oxide minerals make fabulous flashy gemstones.

CUPRITE

The deep crimson crystals of cuprite, known as ruby copper, are some of the rarest and most valuable gems there are. Most of the crystals are too tiny to see, but some form cubes or octahedrons with flat faces.

A major source of copper metal, this mineral is often found alongside native copper, malachite and azurite.

RUTILE

Rutile forms glittery thin needles, which can be red or reddish-brown. They are often surrounded, or swallowed up, by other minerals, such as quartz. Rutile is important as it is the main source of the metal titanium. It also occurs in certain schist and gneiss rocks.

SPOT IT

Look for this metallic mineral in the veins of pegmatite rock.

Rutilated quartz

Rock-tionary

Octahedron – a crystal shape with eight flat faces

SPINEL

Spinel specializes in octahedron-shaped crystals – the classic jewel shape – but also occurs in flattened triangles. Its gorgeous blood-red colour means that it is often mistaken for ruby. In fact, it is often found alongside true rubies, but it also occurs in pink, blue, purple, green, brown, black and clear forms. As it is hard and doesn't scratch easily, spinel makes a perfect gemstone.

SPOT IT

Spinel is common in peridotite rocks.

DID YOU KNOW?

Many famous 'rubies', such as the egg-sized Black Prince's ruby in the Imperial State Crown of the UK, are actually spinel gemstones.

CASSITERITE

Cassiterite is one of only a few minerals that contain tin. Loaded with the dense metal, this mineral feels heavy. Although it mostly occurs as masses of tiny crystals or smooth bean shapes, it can also form amazing metallic pyramid-shaped crystals with worn-looking, flat faces. Pure cassiterite is colourless, but more often than not iron impurities make it a brownish black.

SPOT IT

Search for cassiterite in veins in granite rocks, where you'll find it with quartz, rutile and wolframite.

HYDROXIDE MINERALS

Many hydroxide minerals are formed when water and weather on the Earth's surface cause changes to the make-up of minerals in rocks. These are called secondary minerals, as they form after the original minerals.

GOETHITE

This dark mineral with tiny crystals forms when minerals containing iron, such as pyrite and magnetite, are altered by weathering. It is sometimes called 'iron hat', as it sits on top of iron deposits like a hat. Goethite (say 'gurr-tite' or 'go-thite') is a super common mineral and is generally brown or a dull black.

ROCK SPOTTING TIP

Goethite is a run-of-the-mill mineral; however, some rare specimens have pillows of wonderfully smooth crystals, which look like velvety cushions.

MANGANITE

Another dark grey to black mineral, manganite is an important source of the metal manganese. Crystals of manganite can be rather 'groovy', made up of many long strands or with deep lines marking its blocky faces.

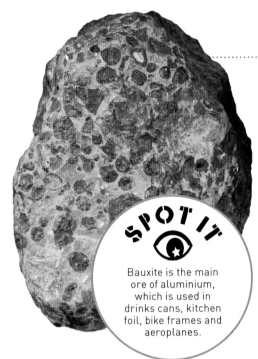

BAUXITE

Bauxite is a strange customer. As the main ore of aluminium, it looks like solidified rice pudding. Bauxite is usually categorised as a mineral, but is actually a soft and crumbly rock. The pea-sized lumps contain a variety of aluminium hydroxide minerals mixed in with clay, quartz and iron oxides.

SPOT IT

Bauxite is the main ore of aluminium, which is used in drinks cans, kitchen foil, bike frames and aeroplanes.

BRUCITE

Found mostly in schist rocks, brucite is a white, pale-greenish or grey-blue mineral. Its crystals are usually flattened plates, thin fibres or tiny lumps. Found with calcite, aragonite and talc, brucite is a soft mineral that can be scratched with a fingernail. It also is a major source of the metal magnesium.

SPOT IT

Brucite is a source of magnesia (magnesium oxide) that is used to calm upset stomachs. Because it is amazingly heat-resistant it is used to fireproof buildings. You can find it in plasterboard.

DID YOU KNOW?

Brucite has a very high melting point, so it is used for lining the insides of potters' kilns. These ovens are used to harden clay pottery at very high temperatures.

HALIDE MINERALS

These brightly coloured minerals are combinations of metals with one of the halogen elements – fluorine, chlorine, bromine or iodine. They are all salts, so they dissolve in water and are left as the 'dregs' when bodies of salty water dry out.

ROCK SALT

This is one stone that is okay to eat. Rock salt – also called halite – is a deposit of the chemical sodium chloride, but we usually just call it salt. Salt has been used for thousands of years to add flavour to food. It can also take the water out of food so that it will last longer without going bad. You can put it on your chips, but too much salt can cause health problems. Rock salt is usually white or colourless, although some forms can be orange, blue or even purple.

SPOT IT

Look for rock salt in massive underground 'salt domes'... or find it in your salt shaker at home.

ROCK SPOTTING TIP

Salt crystals are normally small cubes, but if conditions allow them to grow slowly, they sometimes form large 'hopper crystals'. These look like square cups with stepped sides.

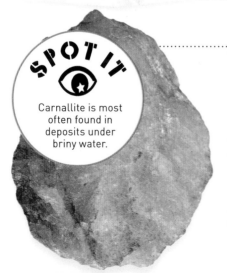

SPOT IT

Carnallite is most often found in deposits under briny water.

CARNALLITE

These salts form in hot places where only a little water flows into a lake or inland sea. As the hot sun dries out the lake some water evaporates, leaving salts in the remaining water, which form solid crystals and drop to the bottom. Carnallite is often found mixed with sylvite and halite. Another soft mineral, carnallite has a greasy sheen, and can be colourless to white, blue, yellow or red.

SYLVITE

This is another salty-tasting mineral. Sylvite is almost identical to rock salt, but it contains potassium chloride, instead of sodium chloride. It is mostly found in cubes or coarse lumps that are soft and easily broken. Sylvite can be colourless to white, but often has shades of blue, yellow or red in its crystals.

SPOT IT

This mineral is often used in low-sodium cooking salt, but its main use is as a fertilizer.

DID YOU KNOW?

Sylvite was first found on the famous Italian volcano, Vesuvius.

FLUORITE

Fluorite is the most colourful mineral in the world. It comes in a rainbow, from purple to green and yellow, and everything in between. You can often see sections of different colours in the same crystal! It is found in the veins of granite rocks, often along with lead and silver ore minerals. Fluorite forms blocky octahedrons and cubes; although it would make a beautiful precious stone, it is just a bit too soft to be worn as jewellery.

DID YOU KNOW?

Fluorite has loads of industrial uses, but the number one is probably steel-making. This mineral lowers the melting point of impurities in iron ore, making them runnier and easier to remove.

MINERALS

CARBONATE MINERALS

Carbonates are a family of soft minerals that come in a range of fantastic colours. Made out of metals combined with carbon and oxygen atoms, they all dissolve in mild acid.

MALACHITE

This sleek, emerald-green mineral has been an important ore of copper since ancient times. Crystals are rare but, if they do form, they occur in clusters of tiny chips. It is more common to find malachite as smooth, opaque stones. Malachite often grows in layers, giving it lovely, glossy green rings when cut.

SPOT IT

Beautiful, banded malachite is used in jewellery and polished beads.

DID YOU KNOW?

Malachite is named after the mallow plant from which marshmallows were originally made.

RHODOCHROSITE

Sometimes called Inca Rose, this beautiful pink mineral is a carbonate of the metal manganese. Rhodochrosite is found in cracks in metamorphic and sedimentary rocks.

SPOT IT

Rhodochrosite is often found alongside minerals containing silver.

MINERALS

SMITHSONITE

Like malachite and rhodochrosite, smithsonite is not normally found as visible crystals, but is mostly discovered as a rounded mass. It has many colours, ranging from off-white and yellow, to apple-green, blue, pink and purple.

BORAX

You might know this mineral as a slime-maker. Powdered borax is a household cleaning product that you can use to make a super-stretchy, springy slime. It occurs naturally in dry regions, where water has evaporated from salty lakes. It is so dry that it often crumbles to dust and is found as a soft and gleaming white powder.

SPOT IT

You may find borax powder in your house. It is used as laundry soap and as a fungus-killing foot soak.

CALCITE

Calcite is a soft, crystal-clear mineral that looks like a chip of ice. This common carbonate mineral is famous for having a huge variety of crystal shapes.

Calcite is the most common naturally occurring form of calcium carbonate, an important mineral in many rocks. This soft mineral is usually white and is mostly made up of squashed, rectangle-shaped crystals. However, calcite is unique for forming lots of different types of crystals. So far, mineral hunters have identified more than 800 different shapes.

Dogtooth spar

Calcite can form large crystals which are often translucent (let light pass through them). These are sometimes called spar. Iceland spar is a crystal-clear form of calcite, which looks like a chip of ice. Other interesting forms include nailhead spar, with flattened lumps on top of thin hexagon-shaped needles, and jagged-edged dogtooth spar.

Iceland spar

Calcite is an essential part of all carbonate rocks. It is found in both sedimentary and metamorphic rocks, such as limestone, chalk and marble. Naturally acidic rainwater dissolves carbonate rocks, hollowing them out to make vast underground caverns, dizzying cliffs and some of the most impressive landscapes on Earth.

Calcite-rimmed pools in the Buchan caves, Australia.

MINERALS

ROCK SPOTTING TIP

Calcite crystals split light rays into two parts, which take different paths through the crystal. One direction is slower than the other, so the light arrives at your eye at slightly different times. If you put a lump of calcite on top of a page in a book, you get a spooky double image.

DID YOU KNOW?

Turn off the lights and give a piece of calcite a sharp tap. You should see a bright blue flash of light. This effect is known as triboluminescence (say 'tri-bow-loom-in-ess-ents').

SPOT IT

Calcium carbonate dissolves in acid, releasing carbon dioxide gas. A sure-fire test for calcite is to drop weak acid onto its surface. If it contains calcite it will fizz on contact.

DID YOU KNOW?

Calcite's trickery with light would make it the ideal material for a light-bending invisibility cloak!

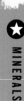

SULPHATE MINERALS

This is a family of soft, pale-coloured minerals. They are formed of sulphate units made up of one sulphur atom joined to four oxygen atoms and combined with different metals. There are more than 200 sulphate minerals, but only three are widespread – gypsum, barite and anhydrite.

GYPSUM

Gypsum is a common mineral that forms in thick, grainy beds. It is soft and comes in tan browns and greys, or can be colourless. Crushed gypsum is used in fertilizer, plaster and cement.

SPOT IT

New Mexico, USA, has sand fields made of blinding-white gypsum grains. These fields are rare because the mineral dissolves in water, so the climate must be bone dry.

ROCK SPOTTING TIP

Like many other sulphate minerals, gypsum often forms in very salty water. Crystals are made naturally in the water and drop to the bottom. The crystal sediments build up into thick deposits.

BARITE

Also called 'heavy spar', barite is the main source of the dense metal barium. It forms in hot springs and is often found along with minerals in limestones containing lead and silver, as well as with haematite. Barite can be colourless, white, pale blue, yellow or brown.

WULFENITE

This pretty lead ore comes in bright orange, red and yellow. It mostly forms crystals that look like thin, flat plates.

ANHYDRITE

Gypsum and anhydrite are very similar minerals and are regularly found together, along with rock salt, in beds that can be hundreds of metres thick. Anhydrite usually forms in rocklike clumps of tiny colourless or pale-coloured crystals. Single large crystals are very rare.

CELESTINE

Celestine has a pretty blue colour and can look a lot like barite, but it doesn't feel as heavy. It is also much rarer.

SPOT IT

Since it contains the chemically reactive metal strontium, powdered celestine is used in fireworks to give a bright red colour.

SULPHATE MINERALS

This bunch of weird and wonderful minerals are beautiful and rare. They contain heavy metals, such as tungsten and molybdenum, and are often valuable ores.

WOLFRAMITE

This mineral has the coolest, most superhero-sounding name. The word 'wolframite' comes from the old word for tungsten. It is the main ore of tungsten, a heavy metal used to make tough armour plating for military vehicles. Its short, dark crystals are usually found in granite and pegmatite rocks, along with other ore minerals such as cassiterite.

SPOT IT

Flawless examples of scheelite crystals are sometimes cut into gemstones.

SCHEELITE

A rare ore of tungsten, scheelite forms small double pyramids called octahedrons. Unlike wolframite, its pale yellow to orange-yellow crystals are translucent.

MINERALS

CROCOITE

The shockingly bright, orange-red crystals of crocoite make it a collector's dream. This rare mineral contains lead and chromium metals and mostly forms in long, thin crystals.

SPOT IT

Crocoite is an ore of chromium metal. You'll find chromium in your stainless steel cutlery and on shiny kitchen appliances.

SPOT IT

Snow-white alabaster has an amazing trick – it seems to radiate light just below its surface. Because of this trait, it was often used to make windows in European churches.

ALABASTER

Alabaster is a pure white form of gypsum. Soft and fine-grained, it looks more like a rock than a mineral. Thanks to its softness, it is great for carving into statues and ornaments.

MINERALS

PHOSPHATE MINERALS

This family of minerals contains the chemical element phosphorus combined with oxygen. Phosphorus is important for living things – each year more than 200,000 tonnes of phosphate minerals are crushed to make crop fertilizer.

APATITE

Apatite is the most common phosphate mineral. It is also called calcium phosphate and forms an important part of most igneous, sedimentary and metamorphic rocks. However, large crystals of apatite are not common; it mostly occurs as tiny, dark chips. Apatite is used in fertilizer, which restocks the soil with minerals that plants use up as they grow.

SPOT IT

You can also find apatite in your body. Calcium phosphate is the hard mineral that builds our teeth enamel and bones.

DID YOU KNOW?

Apatite is a name that covers three different minerals – fluorapatite, chlorapatite and hydroxylapatite. It is difficult to tell these three minerals apart without special equipment.

CARNOTITE

This bright, sickly coloured, radioactive mineral looks like something that could turn you into a comic book superhero. Yellow-green, soft, dry and powdery, carnotite has a high uranium content and is often found as a crust on sandstones.

VANADINITE

Minerals that contain the metal vanadium come in all sorts of bright colours. The barrel-shaped or hairlike crystals of vanadinite are yellow, orange, red or brown.

SPOT IT

Vanadinite is the main source of vanadium, which is mixed with steel to make super-hard tools.

VARISCITE

A rare aluminium phosphate mineral, variscite is found in tightly packed masses of tiny crystals.

SPOT IT

A deep greeny-blue, this pretty rock is often cut and polished for jewellery.

ROCK SPOTTING TIP

Variscite looks a bit like another phosphate mineral – the semi-precious stone turquoise. To make things more confusing, it is often found alongside turquoise. Variscite is generally greener in colour.

Rock-tionary

Semi-precious stone - Gemstones that are not diamond, ruby, emerald or sapphire. Semi-precious stones are not as valuable as the four main gems, because they are more common, less shiny and softer.

MINERALS

67

SILICATE MINERALS

Silicates are the most common type of mineral on the planet. They are made of combinations of silicon and oxygen, along with other chemical elements. With more than 1000 different kinds, they make up 90 per cent of all the minerals in the Earth's crust.

FELDSPAR

These are the most abundant minerals in Earth's rocky crust. There are two main types – the K-feldspars, such as orthoclase, that contain potassium, and the plagioclase (say 'pla-gee-oh-kleyz') feldspars, that contain sodium and calcium. Feldspars are found in most igneous and metamorphic rocks – igneous rocks without feldspar minerals are rare. In sedimentary rocks, they are often broken down to form clay minerals. Feldspars are all harder than glass and their crystals tend to form rectangular blocks.

SPOT IT

The pink to white crystals of orthoclase give granite its pink colour. Plagioclase crystals are usually white or grey.

DID YOU KNOW?

Together, the feldspar minerals make up about two thirds of the planet's crust.

MINERALS

ROCK SPOTTING TIP

One type of rock, called anorthosite, is made of almost 100 per cent pure feldspar. This rock forms the pale mountains of the Moon.

TALC

Talc is officially the world's softest mineral. It is a waxy-looking substance with a wide range of colours, but mostly it is white with streaks of green. Found in metamorphic rocks along with serpentinite, talc feels greasy to the touch and can easily be scratched with a fingernail.

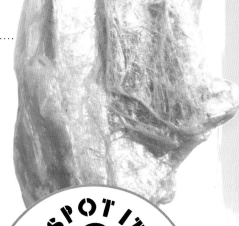

DID YOU KNOW?

Talc is the main mineral of soapstone, a soft, easy-to-carve rock. It is often made into dishes and ornaments.

SPOT IT

Crushed talc makes talcum powder. This puffy stuff is used to dry and perfume feet and to soothe babies' bottoms. A small dusting of talc is used to stop chewing gum from sticking to its wrapper. It is also used to polish grains of rice and to thicken paint.

MICA

Micas are a family of minerals that break into thin, bendy plates. This makes them really easy to spot within rocks. The two most common micas are muscovite and biotite – both are found in many different types of rock, such as granites, pegmatites, schists and gneisses. Biotite is the darker of the pair, with an almost black colour.

ROCK SPOTTING TIP

You can tell mica apart from other similar-looking minerals with a sewing needle – mica is soft enough to be scratched by steel. Use the point of the needle to separate the flaky layers.

QUARTZ

Tiny grains of quartz are the most common material found in sand. Formed by joining silicon and oxygen, this hardwearing silicate mineral is one of the most widespread substances on Earth.

Quartz – like the sand grains it forms – gets everywhere! It is in virtually every igneous rock, particularly those that contain lots of silicon, such as granite, pegmatite and rhyolite. Sandstone is a rock that is almost entirely made from quartz grains. As it is so hard, quartz resists being worn down by wind and weather, and lasts a long time. When older rocks are eroded, the quartz grains they contain are let loose. Transported by water, those mineral grains get deposited on river sandbanks, lakebeds, beaches and on the seabed.

Milky quartz

Quartzite is a metamorphic rock formed of sand grains that have been changed by heat and pressure deep underground. Pure quartz is colourless, but impurities often give it some colour. The most common variety of quartz is milky white, often with dark spots and veins of other minerals running through it. Generally opaque, it has some clear forms. Smoky quartz is transparent grey and often has inclusions. Amethyst is a striking purple variety of quartz, used as a gemstone.

SPOT IT

You look out through windows made of quartz every day – silica sand is the main ingredient in glass.

Clear quartz

Rock-tionary

Inclusion – any material that gets trapped inside a crystal as it forms

DID YOU KNOW?

Sand grains are ancient, perhaps even billions of years old.

Amethyst

ROCK SPOTTING TIP

Many crystals split along lines of weakness, giving them flat faces. Quartz, however, is equally strong in all directions. This means that it breaks unevenly, leaving fracture patterns and rough edges.

Quartz veins in metamorphic rock

A shell-shaped fracture in carnelian quartz

DID YOU KNOW?

Quartz makes up about 12 per cent of the Earth's surface.

MINERALS

71

SILICATE MINERALS

Silicate minerals are formed of silicon atoms surrounded by four oxygen atoms in a pyramid shape called a tetrahedron. There are many ways to join these units together into long chains, so there are lots of different silicate minerals.

JADE

Jolly green jade is a semi-precious stone that has been highly valued since ancient times. The cultures of South East Asia and China produce amazing jade ornaments. In fact, what is known as jade is actually two different silicate minerals – jadeite and nephrite. Both are creamy-white to green stones with microscopic crystals.

DID YOU KNOW?

In ancient China, jade was called the 'stone of heaven' and was thought to give protection from demons.

TOURMALINE

The bright rainbow colours of tourmaline make it one of the prettiest minerals. Glassy-looking tourmalines can be black, green, brown, red, blue, yellow or pink. Many even have two or three colours within their crystals. One of the most striking tourmalines looks like a watermelon, with a red interior and a green outer crust. Crystals can be thin needles or chunky sticks. Tourmaline is found in granite, schist and gneiss rocks.

SPOT IT

Brazil is a famous location for tourmalines. The world's biggest crystal of tourmaline comes from Paraíba, Brazil.

ROCK SPOTTING TIP

There are 11 dazzling varieties of tourmaline.
Some of them are shown below:

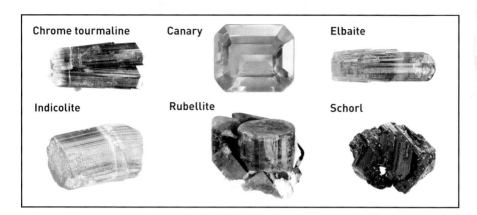

Chrome tourmaline

Canary

Elbaite

Indicolite

Rubellite

Schorl

AUGITE

Augite is one of the most common minerals found in basalts and other dark-coloured igneous rocks, such as gabbro. Its drab, stumpy crystals have rectangular or hexagonal cross sections that end with pyramids.

SPOT IT

It's easy to tell the difference between augite and hornblende. Augite has edges that meet at right angles, while the edges of hornblende crystals meet at 120° and 60°.

HORNBLENDE

Hornblende is another dull, dark mineral with small, squat crystals. The ends of its crystals often look as if they have been broken off. It is because of this and its dusky brownish-green to black colour that hornblende is often mistaken for biotite mica (p69). Hornblende forms an important part of many igneous and metamorphic rocks, especially amphibolite.

MINERALS

73

SILICATE MINERALS

Two related sub-families of silicate minerals are neosilicates and sorosilicates. The neosilicates are tough, hardwearing minerals, many of which are gems and semi-precious stones. The sorosilicates are much rarer than most silicate minerals.

EPIDOTE

Other-worldly epidote looks a bit like kryptonite from the Superman comic books. This lurid green mineral is common in metamorphic rocks. You can often spot it in marbles and schist, where it is a secondary mineral (formed when existing minerals in rocks change with heat and pressure). The crystals have deep grooves in their sides and can sometimes look speckled with several different colours. Good quality transparent stones are cut as jewels.

SPOT IT

Unakite is a rock made up of green epidote mixed with red jasper. Rounded and polished, unakite stones are often used for jewellery or decoration.

DID YOU KNOW?

Epidote crystals have a strange property. When viewed from different angles, they can change colour.

TOPAZ

This gemstone is found in igneous rocks. It is usually colourless or grey, but it can also be pale pink, yellow and light blue. The crystals are often large, and in pegmatite rocks the crystals can weigh hundreds of kilos.

MINERALS

ZIRCON

Zircons are tough little customers. This hard mineral forms in small octahedrons, which are usually golden-brown to orange in colour. Although you may need a magnifying glass to spot the crystals, zircon is very common in igneous rocks. Large blue, green and amber zircons are valuable gemstones.

DID YOU KNOW?

Super tough zircons from the Jack Hills of Australia are the oldest surviving minerals on Earth. They are an estimated 4.4 billion years old.

SPOT IT

Olivine is very easily weathered, so you will often find it looking brown and crumbly on exposed surfaces.

OLIVINE

Olivine is a very common mineral – you'll mostly find it in dark-coloured igneous rocks, such as peridotite and basalt. Glassy and bright green gemstones of olivine are called peridot.

GARNET

The blood-red blips of garnets look a bit like pomegranate seeds embedded in igneous rocks. Garnets are actually an entire sub-family of about 20 different minerals. Other garnets come in a wide range of colours from yellow to blue and purple. Although they are easily cracked, high-quality garnets make beautiful gemstones.

SPOT IT

Small crystals of garnet are ground up to make tough abrasives for polishing metal.

MINERALOIDS

These are the 'not-quite-minerals'. Mineraloids look just like minerals, with their beautiful colours; however, there are a few things that make them different. Many mineraloids are actually made by living things.

ROCK SPOTTING TIP

To be a mineral, a stone needs to tick all the boxes from the flow diagram on p40. But mineraloids look very similar to minerals and may even have one or more of their properties.

PEARL

Pearls are the best known – and most expensive – of all mineraloids. They are made by shelled sea creatures (molluscs). When grit particles drift into a shell and get stuck inside, the mollusc deposits calcium carbonate (the material they use to make their shells) around the grit, creating a hard ball with thin layers like an onion. The layers play tricks with the light, making pearls twinkle.

SPOT IT

Most pearls are made by oysters and are very rare. Experts say look for large, old oysters with wide hinges – the uglier the better!

AMBER

Amber is made from the fossilized resin of ancient pine trees. Time has transformed this sticky substance into a hard burnt-yellow solid. Amber is translucent and you can often see the remains of insects, leaves, seeds, or even frogs and lizards, trapped inside forever.

OPAL

Opal is a glossy stone made of hardened silica gel. It is not a mineral, because it has no fixed pattern of atoms, although precious opals have a more ordered arrangement. The ancient Greeks thought that opals were tears of joy shed by the god Zeus, but we now know that they form inside cracks in rocks when silica-rich water trickles through. Opals can be opaque or translucent.

CORAL

Coral is made of the mineral calcite but is formed entirely by microscopic animals. Corals are colonies of small creatures called polyps, relatives of jellyfish. Each polyp creates a hard little cup for it to sit inside, attached to a rock or another polyp cup. As the colony expands, the coral grows. Although they are tiny, these invertebrates create the biggest biological structures on the planet – coral reefs.

SPOT IT

Coral reefs are usually found in warm, shallow, tropical waters.

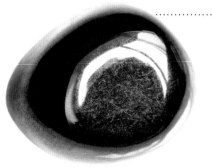

JET

Glossy and sleek, jet is a real black beauty. Although it is often used as a gemstone, it is actually the hardest and most compact form of coal. Jet is made when rotting wood and other plants get buried and squashed underneath tonnes of sedimentary rocks.

DECORATIVE STONES

Some special rocks and stones look drop-dead gorgeous when they are smoothed and polished. Many of these decorative stones have been used since ancient times to make jewellery and ornaments.

Afghanistan is famous for its ancient lapis lazuli mines.

LAPIS LAZULI

For thousands of years, people have desired these deep blue stones. Lapis lazuli is a semi-precious gem, once crushed to make blue colour for paint. Although it's often thought to be a mineral, lapis is actually a rock. This is because, like all rocks, it is made up of a number of different minerals. The most important is a silicate called lazurite, along with calcite, sodalite, pyrite and small amounts of other minerals.

TURQUOISE

Turquoise is a light blue-green, opaque phosphate mineral. Waxy to the touch, its crystals are too small to see without magnification. Turquoise is one of the world's oldest gemstones. It was very important to many ancient cultures, including the ancient Egyptians and the Mesoamerican cultures of Central America, who thought that the stone had special powers.

AGATE

Also called chalcedony, agate is a fine-grained type of quartz made up of microscopic crystals that give it a milky appearance. As it is deposited by mineral-rich fluids moving through rocks, it builds up in layers, giving agate its bands.

ROCK SPOTTING TIP

There are a huge variety of agates. Rainbow agate has intense colours; crazy lace agate has bright colours and wild banding; while moss agate has strands running through it that makes it look like blue cheese.

Crazy lace agate

BLUE JOHN

Blue John is a fluorite with bands of blue, purple, yellow and white. It is found in veins running through limestone rocks. The Romans liked it so much, they made drinking jugs out of it, believing it kept water fresher.

SPOT IT

Blue John is only found in two places – Blue John Cavern and Treak Cliff Hill Cavern, both in the Peak District, UK.

MINERALS

GEMSTONES

Precious and sparkly bright, these four very hard minerals are the most expensive stones on the planet. Nearly impossible to scratch, they maintain their brilliance and shine and have excellent clarity and colour.

DIAMOND

On the face of it, there's nothing special about diamond. It is made of pure carbon, just like coal. However, having been cooked deep within the planet, this material has become radiant, bright and impossible to scratch. It is the hardest known mineral in the world. The only material that will cut diamond is another diamond.

ROCK SPOTTING TIP

Most diamonds are slightly yellow to brown, due to impurities in the crystal. Rough diamonds are often octahedral in shape.

DID YOU KNOW?

One of the largest diamonds ever found was the Cullinan diamond. Discovered in South Africa in 1905, it was 10 centimetres long.

SPOT IT

Non-gem quality corundum is often ground up and used to make sandpaper. It is also used as sandblasting material to clean old, dirty buildings.

SAPPHIRE

Both sapphires and rubies – two of the most precious gemstones in the world – are made of the mineral corundum. Sapphires are generally blue, but they can be any colour from grey or brown to yellow, green and even colour-zoned. The blue colour of sapphires comes from iron and titanium impurities in the crystal.

RUBY

Deep red corundum crystals are called rubies. The colour comes from impurities of chromium metal in the mineral. Rubies range from pale pink to a rich crimson and tend to be small. The rarest and most highly prized are 'pigeon blood' rubies from Burma.

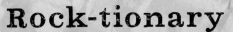

Rock-tionary

Carat – the measurement for the size of gemstones

Some of the most famous emeralds come from mines in the South American country of Colombia. They are often found in granite and pegmatite rocks, mixed in with other minerals, such as quartz.

EMERALD

Emerald has slinky green, hexagonal crystals. These precious stones are the best quality crystals of the mineral beryl. Although they are worth a lot of money, the crystals are often very flawed and shot through with cracks. This makes them difficult – and nerve-racking – to cut!

ROCK SPOTTING EXPERT

Although they have a rich glossy green colour, when scratched on a surface, the powdered emerald dust is white.

MINERALS

FOSSILS

Fossils are the remains of once-living things preserved in rock. They offer a peek into former eras, where unusual plants grew and strange animals wandered the Earth.

TYPES OF FOSSIL

Replacement fossils are parts of an organism turned to stone. Mineral-rich fluids deposit new minerals into the fossil, replacing its body. Fossils can also be made of things that were left behind, like a dinosaur's poo or a footprint. These are called **trace fossils**. Other fossils are made when soft sediment packs around a dead organism, leaving an empty mould, called a **cast fossil**. If just one side of the animal or plant makes an impression, this is called an **imprint fossil**, which often preserves details of skin, bark or leaves.

HOW DO FOSSILS FORM?

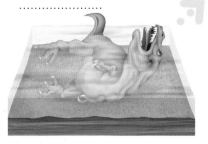

1) An organism dies and its body lies on the ground or at the bottom of the sea. If it remains out of reach of scavengers, it has a much better chance of becoming a fossil.

2) Getting buried quickly under sediment is important – if the organism lies on the surface for a long time, it will rot away, be eaten by scavengers or will be scattered by tides, rain or wind.

DID YOU KNOW?

Ancient people thought that fossils were the remains of mythical creatures that once lived on Earth. Ammonites were called 'snakestones' and dinosaur bones were imagined to be the remains of dragons and giants.

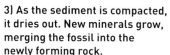

Rock-tionary

Coprolite – a fossilized poo

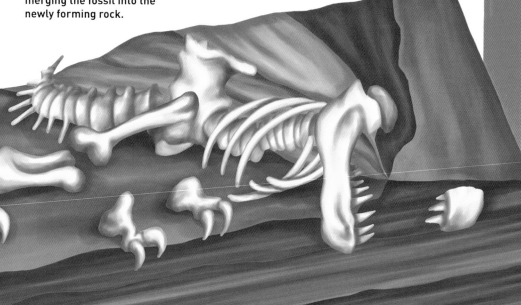

4) Movements within the Earth and erosion of the rock layers eventually bring the fossil to the surface again.

5) The remains must be discovered by someone to become known as fossils.

3) As the sediment is compacted, it dries out. New minerals grow, merging the fossil into the newly forming rock.

INVERTEBRATE FOSSILS

Think of any animal that is not an amphibian, bird, reptile or mammal, and it is an invertebrate. Unlike the vertebrate animals, the invertebrates do not have backbones. Although some live on land, the majority live in the ocean.

TRILOBITES

Once upon a time, these odd-looking creatures were the most abundant animals on Earth. Living under the sea from about 520 million years ago (mya), they looked just like woodlice, with their segmented backs and jointed legs. The biggest trilobite ever found measured 71 centimetres long.

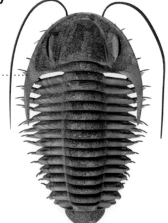

Age: 520–251 mya

CHARNIA

A famous fossil of *Charnia* was found by a schoolgirl called Tina Negus in 1956. It is one of the oldest lifeforms on Earth and scientists are unsure exactly what it was – plant or animal. Although it looks like a leaf print in the rock, there is probably nothing like it alive today.

Age: 579–555 mya

DID YOU KNOW?

The first *Charnia* fossils ever found were small, but some have been discovered that stand taller than an adult human.

GRAPTOLITES

Age: 510–320 mya

These interesting plantlike fossils look like a bunch of squiggles on a rock. There is nothing like them that lives today, so we still aren't sure what they were. The best guess is that each floating seaweed-like strand housed a colony of tiny animals, a bit like coral (p77).

BELEMNITES

Belemnite fossils look like used bullet casings. They are actually the remains of a squidlike creature. The soft body has long rotted away, leaving the hard internal 'sleeve' that gave the animal its shape when it was alive.

Age: 205–66 mya

Age: 530 mya – present

SEA URCHINS

This group of spiny invertebrates includes starfish, brittlestars, sea lilies, feather stars and sea cucumbers. They are easy to spot since, unlike most other animals, they have five-sided bodies.

SPOT IT

Crinoids are sea urchins that look like plants but are actually animals. Sections of their stems form five-pointed stars, known as 'fairy money'.

Age: 410–66 mya

AMMONITES

These curly swirls in rocks are the classic symbol for a fossil. Millions of years ago, ammonites were shelled creatures that swam in warm tropical seas, but they became extinct at the same time as the dinosaurs. The best examples are where the animal's shell has been filled by other minerals during fossilization.

Rock-tionary

Extinct – when a species or group of organisms no longer has any living members on Earth

FOSSIL FISH

Fish have lived in the world's oceans for over 500 million years. While perhaps not as exciting as the dinosaurs, they are some of the best-preserved fossils on Earth.

SPOT IT

Tiny fossils of *Pikaia* are found in just one location – the Burgess Shale in Canada. It is a cute fella, with a small head and a pair of cheeky tentacles.

PIKAIA

Fish were the first vertebrates on Earth. The ancestors of all vertebrates were small fish like *Pikaia*.

Age: approx. 505 mya

JAWLESS FISH

The first fish on Earth looked nothing like today's fish. They were small, had no jaws and were covered in overlapping bony scales. The ancient *Bothriolepis* had a pair of powerful fins that worked like jointed arms to push the fish through mud on the seafloor. Today, there are only two living survivors of this once-large group – lampreys and hagfish, also called 'slime eels'.

Age: 387–360 mya

DUNKLEOSTEUS

This ancient fish was a deep sea terror. Six times longer than the height of an adult human and weighing a tonne, its head was encased in solid bone. Unlike earlier fish, these brutes had snapping jaws, with slicing blades instead of teeth.

Age: 375–359 mya

MEGALODON

Age: 23–2.6 mya

The 'Meg' is thought to be the biggest predator ever to have lived. The stuff of nightmares, this shark may have been up to 18 metres long and weighed over 50 tonnes. The only fossil remains of the Megalodon are teeth and pieces of backbone. The internal skeleton of a shark is made of flexible cartilage rather than hard bone.

SPOT IT

Find fossil shark teeth in Herne Bay, one of the United Kingdom's most popular locations for collecting them.

Rock-tionary

Cartilage – the tough flexible material inside joints and tendons

RAY-FINNED FISH

The fins of these fish are supported by delicate bony spines. Most modern fish belong to this group and they can be found all over the world.

Age: 23–2.6 mya

LOBE-FINNED FISH

The only surviving members of the lobe-finned fish are the air-breathing lungfish and the mysterious deep sea coelacanth. This group is important because their thick, pudgy fins were a starting point for the evolution of four-legged animals.

Age: approx. 370 mya

DID YOU KNOW?

The coelacanth was thought to have gone extinct 100 million years ago. Then in 1938, an expert spotted one in a market in South Africa.

PLANT FOSSILS

Earth is a green planet. The dry parts (and some of the wet bits) are covered in plants which convert the Sun's energy into food, making all other life possible.

LICHENS

The earliest plants were tiny phytoplankton and seaweeds, smaller than the eye can see, living in the oceans. Around 400 million years ago, plants such as lichens and liverworts made the shift onto land. Modern lichens are very similar to these ancient plants.

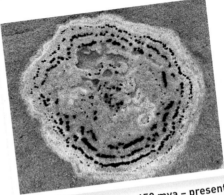

Lichen scars on rock

Age: 450 mya – present

DID YOU KNOW?

There are 1000 times more plants on Earth than animals.

LEPIDODENDRON

Lepidodendron was an enormous fern with a thick, woody trunk. Like all ferns, it spread by producing spores. Also known as giant club mosses, plants like *Lepidodendron* filled prehistoric swamps.

Age: 360–205 mya

SPOT IT

Lepidodendron had diamond-shaped scales that spiralled up its tall trunk.

Rock-tionary

Spore – a tiny single-celled reproductive body, produced by some plants, fungi and single-celled creatures, that can develop into new individuals

GLOSSOPTERIS

Glossopteris was a kind of plant called a cycad that grew very tall. Plants like these were the first to develop seeds that could survive extended dry periods. Flowering plants didn't appear until about 130 million years ago. However, during the age of dinosaurs, *Glossopteris* had some structures similar to modern flowers.

Age: 300–250 mya

SPOT IT

With their distinctive tongue-shaped leaves, *Glossopteris* fossils are easy to spot.

DID YOU KNOW?

Glossopteris fossils are found across all seven continents. This shows that around 200 million years ago, all the world's landmasses were joined together in one giant supercontinent, Pangea.

GINGKO

The gingko tree, sometimes called the maidenhair tree, is known as a living fossil. It is basically the same plant today as it was 270 million years ago.

Rock-tionary

Living fossil – a plant or creature still alive today that looks a lot like its fossils

DID YOU KNOW?

Gingko trees are so tough, they were one of the few living things that survived the atomic bomb blast in Hiroshima, Japan, in 1945.

DINOSAURS

Without a doubt, the most awe-inspiring fossils in the world are those of dinosaurs. These terrifying reptiles ruled the planet for 150 million years, until they died out 66 million years ago.

STEGOSAURUS

The *Stegosaurus*, or 'roofed lizard', is famous for the rows of bony plates that stuck up like tiles down its back, and its tiny skull. This peaceful plant-munching dino was truly a beast of little brain. *Stegosaurus* walked on four legs and had a set of terrifying tail spikes to keep predators away.

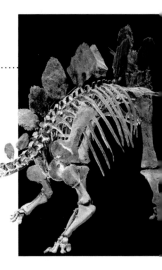

Age: 155–145 mya

DID YOU KNOW?

The vicious spikes on the end of a *Stegosaurus'* tail were nearly a metre long and called a thagomizer.

Age: 68–66 mya

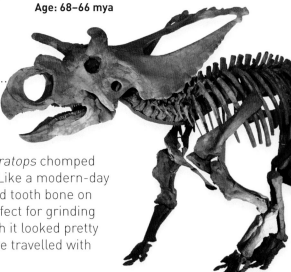

TRICERATOPS

Triceratops is another four-legged vegetarian dinosaur. It had a large skull with a bony frill and three horns on its face. *Triceratops* chomped plants with its horned beak. Like a modern-day elephant, it had one big, fused tooth bone on either side of its mouth – perfect for grinding up tough vegetation. Although it looked pretty grumpy, *Triceratops* may have travelled with others, in small herds.

Age: 150–149 mya

ARCHAEOPTERYX

Fossils of *Archaeopteryx* are probably the most valuable in the world. This unusual dino-bird is halfway between prehistoric dinosaurs and modern birds. Measuring just 50 centimetres long, *Archaeopteryx* had lightweight, delicate bones and flight-ready feathers, just like a modern-day bird. However, it had a bony jaw instead of a beak, a set of pointy teeth, a bony tail and claws on its wings.

TYRANNOSAURUS

With curving teeth up to 23 centimetres long, *Tyrannosaurus rex* was truly the king of the dinosaurs. This ferocious two-legged tyrant lizard was one of the largest predators to ever walk on land. Balancing on two legs with a strong tail, *T. Rex* moved fast and bit hard, with tough, bone-crushing jaws.

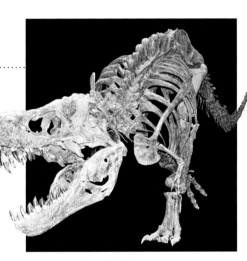

Age: 68–66 mya

DID YOU KNOW?

T-Rex could scoff about 230 kilograms of flesh in one bite.

SPOT IT

The best-preserved *T-rex* skeleton is Sue, an almost complete adult female now kept in the Field Museum of Natural History in Chicago, USA.

FLYING AND MARINE REPTILES

During the age of dinosaurs, giant monsters lurked in the shallow seas and winged creatures soared in the skies. The remains of these remarkable reptiles have made stunning fossils, preserved in rock.

Age: 200–190 mya

DIMORPHODON

Early flying reptiles, such as *Dimorphodon*, had small heads, with short limbs and long tails. The wings of these beasts were made of large flaps of leathery skin stretched between a back leg and a long fourth finger.

PTERODACTYLUS

Pterodactylus was the first pterosaur fossil to be discovered, in 1784. It had a large head, a long neck, long limbs and a short tail.

Age: 200–136 mya

Rock-tionary

Pterosaur – literally meaning 'terror bird', this is a type of flying reptile

SPOT IT

The best place to look for pterodactyl fossils is the Solnhofen limestone of Bavaria, Germany. In the late Jurassic period, this area was a tropical island where many of these creatures lived.

DID YOU KNOW?

The largest pterosaur was *Quetzalcoatlus*, with a wingspan of 10 metres – wider than an F-16 fighter jet.

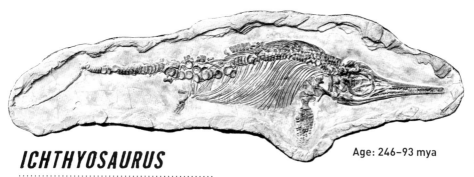

ICHTHYOSAURUS

Age: 246–93 mya

This 'fish-lizard' was dolphin-shaped but had a vertical tail like a shark. Its long snout was filled with lots of sharp, pointed teeth, to snap up fish in the water. Set around the eye socket was a ring of bones to protect the eye in deep water.

PLESIOSAURUS

This long-necked sea creature had the classic Loch Ness monster shape. Swift and agile in the water, they caught fish to eat.

Age: 208–66 mya

DID YOU KNOW?

The largest complete marine reptile ever found was the ichthyosaur *Shastasaurus*. Its body measured 21 metres long – about as long as a right whale.

LIOPLEURODON

Liopleurodon was much smaller than *Shastasaurus*. At nearly 15 metres long, however, it was longer than a modern sperm whale. *Liopleurodon* was known as a pliosaur.

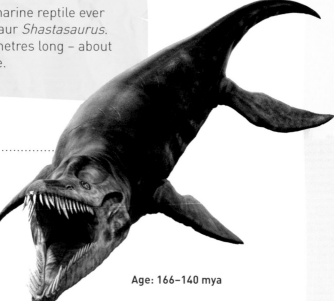

Age: 166–140 mya

GLOSSARY

Angular – sharp-cornered pieces; grains that have not had their edges worn off and rounded

Bedding – layers within a sedimentary rock that make the rock look like a stack of paper

Carat – the measurement for the size of gemstones

Cartilage – the tough flexible material inside joints and tendons

Continent – a solid part of Earth's crust that lies underneath dry land

Crust – the solid rock that covers the surface of the Earth

Crystal – a solid that forms naturally; crystals often have regular shapes with flat faces and clean edges

Crystallize – when crystals start to grow as a substance dries out or cools down

Erosion – the gradual wearing away of a material by the weather or water

Evaporate – when a liquid heats up and turns into a gas

Evaporite – a mineral deposit left behind when a liquid evaporates

Extinct – when a species or organism no longer has any living members on Earth

Fissure – a thin crack in the rocks

Fracture – how a crystal breaks; instead of splitting, crystals often break in shell-shapes

Fragment – a small piece of something

Global warming – the raising temperature across the world due to too much carbon dioxide in the atmosphere; this is largely caused by humans burning fossil fuels

Hopper crystal – a crystal that makes a cup shape, which is thinner at the bottom than the top

Hot springs – hot, mineral-rich waters in volcanic areas

Impurity – a substance that is not usually part of a rock or mineral

Interlocking – when crystals of different minerals grow together and the edges of the crystals meet the edges of others

Intrusion – when hot magma pushes into and between rocks underground

Intrusive – an igneous rock formed by an intrusion beneath the surface

Irregular – a shape that is not even or normal

Living fossil – a plant or creature still alive today that is a lot like its fossils

Magma – hot, melted rock

Mantle – the part of Earth that lies beneath the crust; the mantle is not quite liquid, but it can move and be shaped

Migrate – to move from one place to another

Molten – a solid that has melted to become a hot liquid

Nodule – a lump of a particular mineral embedded inside a rock

Opaque – something that is not see-through

Ores – rocks or minerals that contain valuable metals

Organic – a substance or material that comes from a living (or once-living) organism

Outcrop – a rock formation visible at Earth's surface

Petrification – the process of something turning into stone

Pliosaur – a short-necked marine reptile

Porphyroclast – stretched crystals surrounded by finer mineral grains

Precipitate – when a solid substance is chemically deposited out of a liquid solution

Pterosaur – a type of flying reptile

Silica – also called silicon dioxide, this is one of the most common substances on Earth; it has many forms, but mostly exists as quartz

Solution – a liquid containing dissolved minerals

Spore – a tiny, single-celled body, produced by some plants and fungi, that can develop into new individuals

Streak – the colour of a mineral when powdered; find a mineral's streak by scratching it on a streak plate

Tectonic plate – a thick slab of Earth's crust, carrying continents and oceans; plates drift around the planet's surface, sometimes bashing together at their edges

Thagomizer – the vicious spikes on the end of Stegosaurus' tail

Translucent – letting some light pass through

Vein – a rock fracture that has been filled in by other minerals; veins are often a different colour and texture

Vertebrate – animals that have vertebrae, or backbones

Volcanic – anything relating to volcanoes

Weathering – the slow breakdown of a rock at the surface, by the weather, running water or plants

INDEX